DEDICATION

I would like to dedicate this book to Pastor Philip Miles,
an amazing man of God and an example of faith and mercy.
I pray that one day I may experience God
in the way Philip experiences Him now.
As we continue to travel to places like Egypt,
Australia, New Zealand, and beyond,
I pray that Philip and I would continue to grow
in love with people and ultimately with God.

Divine Romance: How God Draws Us Nearer to Him
by Jeff Vines
Copyright © 2017 College Press Publishing Company
Since 1959, publishers of resources for preachers, teachers,
and Bible students
www.collegepress.com
Order toll-free 800-289-3300

DIVINE
ROMANCE

How God Draws Us Nearer to Him

JEFF VINES

COLLEGE PRESS

Joplin, Missouri

TABLE OF CONTENTS

ACKNOWLEDGMENTS

No work of this nature comes without sacrifice. Sacrifice not merely from the author but from those who know him, work with him, and especially from those in his immediate family. My wife, Robin, and my children, Delaney and Sian, have always encouraged me, in fact challenged me, to record my thoughts concerning spiritual formation. I owe a debt of gratitude to each of them. Without their constant encouragement these ideas would be nothing more than random thoughts floating through the air never settling down in a structured manner on the pages of this book.

I would also like to thank Sandra Dimas who edited this challenging work. Any author knows the value of finding an editor that can strip away all of the chaff until the wheat springs forth and the beauty of wheat fields begin to reflect the glory of God. Sandra is the editor for whom I have been searching for many years. Thank you Sandra!

I need to thank my friend Ravi Zacharias who from the very first time he met me encouraged me to pursue God and to communicate the truth of His word. I have tried to do that since the age of thirty and will continue to do so as long as God gives me breath and life on this beautiful planet that continues to reveal His desire for a divine romance between Creator and Creature.

Finally, to the Elders of Christ's Church of the Valley, the church I serve as Lead Pastor, I say a heartfelt thanks. Thank you for seeing the value of sending me away from the grueling cycle often associated with pastoring a mega church and encouraging me to quieten my spirit and listen to the leading and guiding of the spirit of the living God. Thank you for allowing me to visit Thailand where most of the words on these pages were first recorded. Thank you for investing not merely in CCV but in all those who will read the pages of this book.

FOREWORD
By Dave Stone

Jeff Vines never met a person or a question that he did not find intriguing. You may have had your personal faith and witness bolstered by reading his popular book, *Dinner With Skeptics*. What a helpful resource that was. Jeff challenged skeptics and encouraged seekers to consider the Christian worldview. The premise is/was simple, that it is the only coherent system capable of addressing life's most penetrating questions.

However, in Jeff's new work, *Divine Romance*, he turns the tables on himself as he desperately tries to make sense of the seemingly arbitrary tragedies that have overwhelmed and debilitated so many of his friends and acquaintances. While the Christian may be able to give a satisfactory explanation for the origin of pain and suffering, coming to terms with the varying degrees of individual tribulation is extremely difficult. After all, why does it appear that God has a tragic plan for some lives while many others remain unscathed? For some, no amount of promises or principles will heal their hurts or salve their wounds. In fact, addressing the problem of pain strictly from a philosophical perspective trivializes personhood and often deepens the emotional injuries of the victim.

Imagine spending thirty years traveling the world encouraging tens of thousands of people during the deepest, darkest times of their lives only to discover that words of certainty spoken in the past cannot sustain the darkest night of your soul in the present. Where would you turn? How would you respond? For Jeff Vines, such devastating circumstances catalyze a journey that questions everything he thought he knew about God. Every platitude of encouragement spoken, every positive word espoused, and every philosophical argument presented demanded relentless scrutiny. Attempting to harmonize the goodness and mercy of God with the trials and tragedies of life is both taxing and frightening.

What if there is no God?

What if the best explanation is that there is no explanation?

What if an honest intellectual journey leads to the discovery that life has no meaning, purpose, or hope?

I've always had great respect for Jeff Vines as a preacher and author. But after reading *Divine Romance* somehow my admiration for him has grown. Let me explain… In the past I've always appreciated and loved my friend Jeff because of his victories, but now, even more so, I love and appreciate him because of the valleys he's experienced. You see, there's not a one of us who can't relate to the low points of life (sometimes even better than the mountain top experiences).

In the pages that follow, Jeff pulls back the curtain and gives us a peek into his own personal journey. Such vulnerability is rare these days. I am confident that in a variety of ways his story will intersect with yours. In this book Jeff individually comes to terms with the God of the Bible, whose primary mission is to capture hearts and minds through whatever means necessary. He wants to fill the void that forever haunts your soul. He wants to compel you into the relationship for which you desperately long. That remains God the Father's primary objective for His sons and daughters.

The question is: How far is God willing to go to save us from ourselves?

When you read this book that question will be answered. You'll find far more than trite statements and clichés. Instead you will glean insights from Jeff's own personal pain and struggles with a mental disorder that no one was aware of. If you have lived through extreme challenges and suffered great loss along the way, *Divine Romance* will allow you to discover hope and encouragement. Jeff shows us how each individual revelation must be placed into the greater context of God's overarching objective. Once this primary objective is clearly understood, beauty, pattern and design will begin to emerge out of the chaos of your life.

Reading this book may challenge and frustrate you at times, but I encourage you …keep pouring over it. You'll mine nuggets of wisdom throughout it. And when the dust settles and the fog lifts, every perplexing thought placed into the funnel will come pouring out with purpose and meaning. Confusion will be replaced by clarity, anxiety will be overwhelmed by peace, and depression will be overtaken with a confidence that enables you to live above all the circumstances of life… no matter what you encounter.

So dive in and keep reading, keep seeking understanding. If you do, you'll learn all that lies beyond the beckoning light at the end of the long, dark tunnel. Come to think of it, you'll probably discover the same thing that Jeff did…that the God of the universe is both powerful and personal, whether you are on the mountain top or down in the valley.

Dave Stone, Senior Pastor
Southeast Christian Church
Louisville, Kentucky

INTRODUCTION

Going through the Motions

I'll never forget the day my twenty-year-old daughter looked me straight in the eye and said, "Dad, you don't really care about me."

"What on earth are you talking about?" I asked, shocked by the accusation.

"You talk to me, but you don't really listen," she said. "You go through all the right motions and say all the right things, but it's not because you really mean them; it's because by saying them you make yourself feel better."

My daughter, Sian, has always been a straight shooter with little tolerance for dilly dally. She has also been the apple of my eye from the time she was a little girl. I prayed for her physical and spiritual health, for her future husband, for everything that is possible for a father to pray concerning his daughter. I was intentional in speaking into her life words that would catalyze an independent, confident, God-fearing young woman. I told her she was beautiful so she would not seek a man's approval. I told her she could accomplish anything she sets her mind to so she would never doubt herself. I told her God loves her and will always be with her so she would know where her strength comes from.

In my mind, our relationship was ideal. But the sincerity in her voice squelched my defensiveness and replaced it with a deep sense of sadness. Though it pained me to hear it, I knew she was speaking the truth. Sian's words helped me realize that the way I had been with her reflected how I showed up in most of my relationships. I preferred superficiality—a lot of acquaintances but no real, genuine friendships.

I would discuss other people's problems and issues, but I was afraid to let people know the real me. What if they reject me? What if they don't like the real me?

When the reality sank in that my relationship with my daughter was superficial, I was shattered. I knew I loved her more than life itself, but I also knew I had failed to demonstrate this reality. I decided right then and there that I needed to change if I wanted to give my daughter the deeper relationship for which she longed. The deeper relationship for which I also longed.

✦ ✦ ✦ ✦ ✦ ✦ ✦ ✦ ✦ ✦

We all long for deeper relationships with those we love, whether those relationships are with our spouse, our children, our friends, or extended family. How much more so does God long to be in deeper relationship with us? Just as a young man pursues the woman he loves in hopes of a marriage covenant, so too does God pursue us so that we might become the bride of Christ. This is the divine romance. God does not merely want to bring us into His presence, He wants us to grow in deep community with Him. If God did not spare His own son so that we could come near to Him, how much more will He do to move us beyond superficiality into a deep, intimate relationship where we know Him the way He knows us?

When this reality wholly registers within your spiritual constitution, your life will change dramatically. You will love God with all your heart, soul, mind, and strength (Mark 12:30). You will have other loves, but none like Jesus. You will have other goals and objectives, but only one ultimate objective: "to attain the full measure of the fullness of Christ" (Ephesians 4:13). As you grow in maturity, you will stop pursuing God for the purpose of attaining false idols—money, relationships, power, and prestige. You will stop going through all the right motions and saying all the right things to make yourself feel better. Instead, you will sincerely pursue God for the purpose of truly knowing Him and experiencing Him in a way you never thought possible. In short, He will become the end of all pursuits. As a result, joy will become central to your life and sorrow merely peripheral. You will still experience moments of heartbreak and sadness, but they will be viewed from the perspective of eternity and the world that is yet to come.

This kingdom mindset is perhaps the most powerful byproduct of seeing God as He truly is. The way you look at all pain and suffering will change significantly. A transformation you never thought possible will occur, and there will be no turning back. Not only will you find the contentment, love, and acceptance you have been searching for all of your life, but you will become someone people go to when in physical, spiritual, and emotional turmoil. Those who know God reflect His glory and tend to live such compelling lives that those on the outside looking in begin to gravitate toward them. They want to know the source of such peace and contentment.

So, do you really want to know God the way He seeks to be known? Do you want to experience things you never thought possible? Then keep reading. Like any other relationship, your relationship with God requires going beyond superficiality toward a deeper connection.

As you read through this book, my prayer is that you may indeed discover God, the Creator and Sustainer of all that is, and the One who longs for a deep, intimate relationship with you. But let me give you a warning. Times of life-changing illumination seldom come as a result of information that has been dispensed in simplicity. The "keep it simple stupid" approach to communication may lead to quick and easy insights, but, deep, profound, eternal discoveries require wading through the muck and mire of everyday philosophies venturing into previously undiscovered regions of thought that eventually lead to lands where truth can begin to shine like the sun. Stay the course. The destination is worth the journey.

CHAPTER 1

The Truth About Following Jesus: Let's Just Get It Out There!

Growing up in East Tennessee I dreamed of one day living on the west coast. California represented freedom, excitement, and endless possibilities. The dream became reality in 2008 when Robin and I were offered the opportunity to lead Christ's Church of the Valley, a mega church just thirty minutes east of downtown Los Angeles. I truly love LA! The beaches, mountains, hiking trails, biking paths, and outstanding golf courses appeal to the outdoorsman in me, and, the weather, wow! Can it really get any better than this? However, the first few years catalyzed a rather intense culture shock. Driving is the biggest challenge by far. Due to LA's eclectic population, multiple races from multiple countries occupy the motorways. Everyone drives by the rules associated with their country of origin. This makes for an exciting commute to and from work when the highways are at their most crowded. Most drivers, despite what you may hear or read, are courteous and cultured and are quite willing to share the road with everyone else in a civilized and often welcoming manner. However, there are those who can become quite overwhelmed with the mass humanity and feel the need to escape. Unfortunately, one's move toward self-centeredness can become contagious and suddenly, boys with toys begin to assert themselves, weaving in and out of lanes, cutting other drivers off or refusing to merge in an orderly fashion. Suddenly, all hell breaks loose and someone shouts at someone else and then next thing you know, fisticuffs!

Then of course, there are the earthquakes. Never had one of those in Tennessee (except the first time I saw Robin Delaney) but that's an earthquake of a different kind. My first earthquake was a 5.8 roller in the middle of the day. While seated at Corner Bakery with two workmates enjoying a quiet lunch, the pavement began to shake before the carpark began to roll toward me. This was truly a rather unsettling experience. My friend Jon who has lived in LA most of his life never even moved. He just sat there "taking it like a man" as if he had experienced hundreds of these bothersome shakes before. The local football coach on the other hand, you know the type, the self-proclaimed tough guy, stood up in panic and said, "It's an earthquake! Run man, run!" To which my friend Jon calmly replied, "Why? It's just an earthquake!"

I'll have to admit, that was a type of culture shock I had not experienced in New Zealand nor Africa. Earthquakes aside, I love LA! Yes, I am often challenged by a culture with which I am unfamiliar. But I love the diversity of the population, the plethora of music and art, and quite frankly, the love for life most Angelenos possess.

As a pastor, I've seen a troubling pattern developing in churches over the last twenty-five years. When people come to Christ and enter the church they experience a culture shock similar to the one I experienced above. Seldom do new Christians come into the church with eyes wide open or a full vision of what it means to follow Jesus. As they move deeper into their relationship with Christ, a sort of culture shock rocks their world when suddenly they realize that rather than God existing for their purposes, they actually exist for His. While it is true that many come to God because all other efforts have failed, the God to whom they are drawn is often one they have created in their own image, or one that has been shaped by an affluent culture looking to gain access to the earthly riches found in Christ Jesus. From televangelists who promise health, wealth and prosperity to mega church pastors who often omit the more difficult aspects of discipleship and the call to "die" to oneself, the Christian community has often engaged in a type of apologetic that tickles people's ears catalyzing a spiritual buzz proclaiming what people want desperately to hear rather than telling them the truth that "in this world you will have trouble" (John 16:33). Indeed, in our world, we tend to gravitate toward passages like John 14:14, "You may ask me anything in my name, and I will do it," while fleeing anxiously away from passages like Matthew 16:24, "Whoever wants to be my disciple must deny themselves and take up their cross and follow me."

Or maybe the shock comes from all the fake Pollyanna Christians who pretend everything is fine but are hiding dark secrets or deep pains. Whatever the cause may be, when people come to Christ and ultimately to church, they expect God to reward them with health, wealth, and a problem-free life devoid of any hardship—but that is not what happens! Discipleship looks far different from a perfect life. Not everyone's faith is real, but if it is, I promise you that there will be conflict in your life.

Just look at the lives of Shadrach, Meshach, and Abednego. Theirs is an old and familiar story but a good one nonetheless. They truly love God with all their heart, soul, and strength. They are genuine believers living in an unbelieving world. Detailed in Daniel 3, Shadrach, Meshach, and Abednego's narrative depicts three devoted men living in Babylon under the rule of King Nebuchadnezzar, a king who desperately wanted to unify his kingdom under one all-encompassing religion. No better way to galvanize a people than to bring them together under one religious ideal. While this may not cause much conflict in the dominant polytheistic cultures of the day, Shadrach, Meshach, and Abednego would have been greatly offended by the proposal. They held a firm conviction that only the one true God, YAHWEH, is worthy of worship and, to bow down to any other God was in fact, blasphemy!

Nevertheless, King Nebuchadnezzar made an image of gold 90-feet high and 9-feet wide and demanded that everyone worship the golden image or risk being thrown into a blazing furnace (Daniel 3:4-6). To the monotheistic trio, such a command placed them in a rather precarious position. They had tried desperately to remain loyal to Yahweh without separating themselves from the culture holding them captive. In other words, they had not assimilated but neither had they separated. They remained "in" the culture without being stained by it. They lived distinctly as God-followers, illuminating the light of Jehovah into a dark world. The trouble with lights however is that they often, although inadvertently draw attention to themselves. It was only a matter of time before two opposing worlds would collide and an ensuing wave of conflict would come crashing down on Shadrach, Meshach, and Abednego.

King Nebuchadnezzar was furious when these young men wouldn't worship his image of gold. So he heated the furnace seven times hotter and "commanded some of the strongest soldiers in his army to tie up Shadrach, Meshach and Abednego" (Daniel 3:20). But a funny thing happened on the way to incineration! The king says (in verse 25), "Look! I see four men walking around in the fire, unbound and unharmed, and the fourth looks like a son of the gods." What? The fire didn't kill them or harm them. The blaze did not scald, boil, or fry them. In fact, the only thing the fiery furnace burned were the ropes that bound Shadrach, Meshach, and Abednego. In a fiery conflict, they had discovered true freedom. Once you have been through a fiery furnace, every other threat looks rather benign by comparison.

The point is that even though Shadrach, Meshach, and Abednego resolved to live a quiet and peaceable life, conflict came. Why? If your faith is real, conflict is certain. It might not be of fiery-furnace proportions, but you can be certain that your life of faith will challenge cultures that are moving in the opposite direction. A life that lives against the grain and swims upstream will sooner or later bump into those who are caught up in the vortex of a world system that rejects the one true God. In fact, if you never experience conflict, never take a stand for anything, and no one ever belittles you, I have to ask you, is it because you've compromised your faith and assimilated into your culture? Have you blended into Babylon to such a degree that there are no visible distinctions in your life? The God of the Bible not only changes what you do but what you want to do. If that has not happened, you've assimilated into a Godless culture and therefore warrant no opposition.

In Luke 6:26 Jesus said, "Woe to you when everyone speaks well of you." This doesn't mean that it's okay to invite people to speak ill of you because you're being rude and obnoxious. Don't be that person who goes into a public place and tells everyone that God hates sinners, homosexuals, and Muslims. If you do that then of course no one will speak well of you. You're an obnoxious, unloving, uncaring pain in the posterior! Yet, if you never experience conflict between your world view and the world view of those not following Jesus, then, you have probably compromised your faith, assimilated into the culture, and are pursuing foreign gods.

✦ ✦ ✦ ✦ ✦ ✦ ✦ ✦ ✦

Every Friday night it was the same question, "Hey Jeff, you want to get drunk and get naked?" While living and working in Zimbabwe, Africa, my friend Tim greeted me with this question every Friday afternoon. Our weekend pursuits were obviously quite different at the time. For years, Tim struggled with my pursuit of purity where women were concerned. In his mind, this was a waste of youth and manhood. But as often is the case, Tim's carefree living never yielded the freedom for which he longed. Instead, years of living in the flow of the world had yielded broken hearts, broken dreams, and a broken man. In the midst of this, Tim discovered a relationship with Jesus and never looked back. Once Tim submitted to Christ, everything fell into place, right?

Last year, during my annual trip to Rwanda to preach in the prisons, I diverted to Zimbabwe to pay my old friend Tim a visit. I hadn't seen him in fifteen years. He greeted me with both laughter and tears as we reminisced about old times and talked about the years we had been apart. As we made our way into his office at the Borrowdale Golf Club, Tim shared how his life changed since he came to faith.

"Jeff, I never told you this," he said, "but it has taken me fifteen years to get my head above water financially, and to feed my wife and kids after I became a Christian."

"How did this happen?" I asked.

Tim explained that, when he became a believer, he lost his job at a prestigious golf club because he refused to participate in unethical business practices. Then he was fired from another golf job because he refused to teach only European kids. His heart and passion for young black golfers was not appreciated. He was fired yet again when he refused to sneak golfing equipment into South Africa without paying the government duty. "I wanted to do the right thing. Because of that, I lost everything, one job after the next," he said. He continued, explaining that he had lost all of his business contacts and most of his friends because he refused to participate in illegitimate business practices.

I shook my head in disbelief. After a moment of allowing it all sink in, I asked him, "Tim, would you do it again?" His response was deeply profound. "Yes, I would. With each temptation to give in to their illegitimate schemes came a deeper conviction to honor God. Over time as I passed test after test I began to realize that my faith was indeed real." In other words, Tim refused to assimilate into a culture that required him to violate his commitment to Christ, no matter what it cost him personally. In fact, Tim lost everything for his faith, and it took him fifteen years to recover from the financial losses he and his family endured. Let's just go ahead and get it out there. Conflict has a way of revealing who or what you really love, to whom or what you are truly committed, and who or what is the ultimate object of your affection.

Like Shadrach, Meshach, and Abednego, Tim decided that he would choose God above all else. Is that you? If that's you then you're going to choose God above and beyond that relationship that you're in right now that you know full well is not from God. When you get serious about pursuing God, you will cease all illegitimate relationships and business practices. You will stop cheating your boss, stop sleeping with your girlfriend, stop rationalizing your immoral behavior and resolve to love

God with all your heart, soul, mind, and strength.

You must decide who is going to be your god. Is it money? Success? Material possessions? Jesus said, "You cannot serve both God and money" (Matthew 6:24b). What is the thing you're involved in that may be perfectly acceptable but because you're so consumed with it, has become a god in your life? It is destroying your relationships with your spouse, children, family, and friends? Know that you won't have merely one showdown with the fiery furnace and that's it. You are going to face it every single day with offers and opportunities to make small compromises or hold your ground. Those faith trials and conflicts are either going to validate you as a legitimate, fully devoted follower of Jesus, or expose you for the pretender that you really are. But make no mistake, if your faith is real, conflict will come.

But take heart. If your faith is perpetual, confirmation will also come. God knows whether your faith is eternal and lasting, but He wants to make sure you know it too. So guess what God does? He puts you in situations where your faith can be confirmed, and then you will develop a quiet resolve. When trials come and you are victorious through Jesus, you will know that you're the real deal; your faith will be validated and strengthened.

Our response to all conflict will be determined by our reason for living. If your reason for living is self-preservation, then when God sends you into the furnace you're going to kick and scream accusing God of abandonment and apathy. But if your reason for living is to glorify God with your life, which is what a fully devoted follower of Jesus does, then even though the flames are painful and it hurts, you submit to the fire because ultimately you know you are living for a purpose greater than yourself, and although you would prefer a furnace-free life, you trust that God is able to do much more than you could ever ask or imagine in the midst of the fire.

✦ ✦ ✦ ✦ ✦ ✦ ✦ ✦ ✦

There is no better example of this steadfast purpose than the life of missionary Jim Elliot. Before Elliot came on the scene international missionaries were often "ministry misfits" who struggled to fit into U.S. ministries. Jim Elliot, however, was a respected pastor, an excellent teacher, and gifted writer. People thought he might become the next Billy Graham, setting the world on fire with the gospel. However, Jim tended to avoid praise and adoration drawn instead to a life lived for an audience of One. Early in his life he felt God calling him to take the gospel to an unreached people group in Ecuador—the Auca Indians. He longed to take the love of Christ, the message of salvation, and the promise of eternal life to a people who had not yet heard the name, Jesus.

Jim, along with his wife Elisabeth and four other missionary families, left all they owned behind and immigrated deep into the South American jungle. After months of prayer and sacrifice, Jim and his four associates began making regular flights in a single-engine airplane over the village of the Auca Indians dropping gifts as peace offerings hoping to open the lines of communication and dispel any suspicion of hostility. After relentless efforts to convince the Auca Indians of their peaceful intent, Jim and the other missionaries swooped down closer landing on the carefully constructed airstrip situated on the outskirts of the Auca village. They landed, set up camp, and soon made contact with the Indians. Jim said the few words he knew in their language. Words that he had practiced over and over and over again: "I am your friend." Unfortunately, the Aucas remained unconvinced and vigorously speared the five young men to death. (Their lives are depicted in the movie *End of the Spear*.)

In her book *Shadow of the Almighty*, Jim's widow Elisabeth Elliot quotes from her husband's journal: "He is no fool who gives what he cannot keep to gain that what he cannot lose."

After losing her husband, Elisabeth Elliot returned to the jungles of South America with her eight-year-old daughter to minister to the very tribe of indians responsible for her husband's demise. In her book *Keep a Quiet Heart*, she tells of finding the man who killed her husband and leading him to Jesus, the Savior who says, "I am your friend." An entire village of people came to Christ because one man and his wife lived by this code: even if he does not spare my life, I will do what He's asked me to do. Though conflict may come, I will serve Him. Though my life does not turn out the way I had hoped and planned, I will forever follow Him.

Let's just get it out there! Nowhere in the Bible are we promised an easy life. In fact, we are promised conflict. We are from another world. We live here but we are citizens of another place. Yes, God often opens the windows of heaven and pours out His blessings on us, but, there are also times of conflict and tension and war. In these times we are called upon to endure for the sake of His kingdom and to trust in the world that is yet to come.

Elizabeth writes:

> "Heaven is not here, it's there. If we were given all we wanted
> here, our hearts would settle for this world rather than the next.
> God is forever luring us up and away from this one, wooing us to

Himself and His still invisible Kingdom, where we will certainly find what we so keenly long for."

Jim's life sparked a whole new missionary movement. Highly gifted, multi-talented men and women began immigrating overseas to places like Asia, Africa, South America and Eastern Europe for the express purpose of taking the Gospel to the world. Today, twelve million Bibles are printed every year in the underground movement in Asia and Eastern Europe. Missionary movements like Pioneer Bible Translators and Wycliffe, catalyzed by the life and sacrifice of Jim Elliot, continue to strive diligently in their efforts to reach the unreached.

Because Elisabeth lived with eternity in mind, she was able to stay devoted to kingdom work when her faith was tested. She knew what most of us still need to learn—that God's primary objective in the world is to expand His kingdom and that He reserves the right to use anyone however He sees fit to accomplish that end—even if that means pain or conflict coming into your life. The legitimate, authentic follower of Christ who understands this truth raises their hands to the heavens and says, "Here I am Lord, send me!" If God told you that an entire unreached people group would be saved if you would be willing to die, would you do it?

✦ ✦ ✦ ✦ ✦ ✦ ✦ ✦ ✦

The story of Shadrach, Meshach, and Abednego shows us the ultimate test of authenticity. In Daniel 3:17–18 they tell the king, "If we are thrown into the blazing furnace, the God we serve is able to save us from it, and he will deliver us from Your Majesty's hand. *But even if he does not*, we want you to know, Your Majesty, that we will not serve your gods or worship the image of gold you have set up" (emphasis added). God is able to save you from pain, but that does not mean He is obligated to do so. Yes, He could have helped you pass that test, secured that job for you, saved your marriage, healed your mother, but He didn't. While God can do all things, He isn't obligated to do all things and the truth is that He seldom does what we think He should.

When Cassie Bernall looked down the barrel of a gun during the Columbine shootings and was asked, "Are you a Christian?" she said, "Yes." They killed her. In a church video a few weeks earlier, Cassie had confessed, "I just try not to contradict myself, to get rid of all the hypocrisy and just live for Jesus Christ." Wow! Cassie did the right thing…and paid for it! This is the type of culture shock that sometimes causes people to walk away from God.

There are two assumptions we make that are poor measuring rods for the fully devoted follower of Christ. The first is the more-good-than-bad mindset. Too many Christians still follow the gospel of moralism believing that "good works" guarantees salvation. The thought is: If I have more good in my life than bad, then the scales are in my favor and God will accept me into heaven in the end. Such a scenario tends to overestimate personal goodness and underestimate the holiness of God.

The second misconception is closely related. The assumption is that if you do what is right, God will protect you from pain and hardship. "Being good" grants you salvation in the future and divine protection in the present. Those who live by this precept subconsciously believe that if they do what is right they place God in a sort of binding contract where God is required to prevent the possibility of painful experiences. While this type of theology may grant a person a temporary sense of security, it's only a matter of time before the fires of the furnace light up. Notice one more time: Shadrach, Meshach, and Abednego were suffering for doing the right thing! They refused to bow down to the false god and that earned them a one-way ticket to the fiery furnace.

To you and me, there is a lack of justice in this story. Those three men honored God, so He should have saved them from the furnace, right? The problem is you cannot harmonize the teaching of a health, wealth and prosperity gospel with passages like John 21, where Jesus tells Peter that he is going to suffer a great deal, and there will come a time when he will stretch out his hands (be crucified). Peter was crucified, and his death glorified God. The church began to spread like wildfire, and the early church fathers wrote, "The church was planted by the teaching of the Apostles like Peter, and watered plentiful with the blood of the saints."

First Peter 4:19 says, "So then, those who suffer according to God's will, should commit themselves to their faithful Creator, and continue to do good" (NIV). What? It could be God's will that I go into the furnace? Yes. Don't let safety and security become your god. Don't desire safety and security over and above God's call on your life, but instead, risk it all for His purposes. Continue to do the good, even when you realize it's going to cost you everything. Can you do that? Will you do that?

Our response to pain will be determined by our reason for living. If your reason for living is self-preservation, then when God sends you into the furnace you're going to kick and scream. But if your reason for living is to glorify God with your life, which is what a fully-devoted follower of Jesus does, then even though it's painful and it hurts, you submit to the flames of the fire because ultimately you know you are living for a purpose greater than yourself.

To suggest that God is unloving, or is not real just because He didn't do what you think He should have done, is to assume that God's wisdom is limited to that of your own. But God has the ability to see every event from every possible angle. Only He sees how every event is connected to every other event. Furthermore, he knows the psyche of every human being. He knows how each person is wired and what will draw them into the one thing he wants most for them. Yes, God knows what you want, but He also has all of eternity in mind and will make the best decision so that the ultimate goal can be accomplished—Divine Romance.

God had the ability to save Shadrach, Meshach, and Abednego long before they were ever thrown into the fiery furnace. He could have slain all the guards before they had a chance to tie up or bind these three young men. Had God wanted, He could have destroyed the statue and put an end to King Nebuchadnezzar's reign long before the council passed such an unholy edict. Why didn't He? Only God knows. The reality however is that the same statements could be made concerning your own personal conflicts. God could stop them long before they eventuate into reality. Or, He could provide an escape hatch rescuing you from the possibility or likelihood of any trouble. Why doesn't He? Perhaps God needs the furnace to burn the ropes that are presently binding you. Maybe He wants you to know that your faith is genuine. Maybe He wants others around you to know that you are the real deal and there truly is another kingdom that is worth living for. Let's just get it out there in the open. If you live for God, conflict is going to come. When you obey the call of God, it will be difficult. When you answer the call of God to leave everything behind and move to the jungles of South America the only promise you have is that God will do much more than you could ever hope for or imagine. God often does His best work in you when your world falls apart and the only hope you have is that Jesus will show up and reveal Himself in a way you have never seen before. These types of "Jesus revelations" are the very things that will ultimately draw you into the kind of relationship God ultimately wants with you.

A pastor in our church shared a powerful story with me. There was a time in his life when he became very depressed. Getting out of bed was such a challenge. A typically jovial and fun-loving kind of guy suddenly lost interest in all the things that used to bring him so much joy. No one could explain what was happening to him. Depressed, despondent, and downtrodden, my friend was ready to throw in the towel and take his chances in the next life. At the end of his rope, He got on his knees and prayed, "By the power that you raised Jesus from the dead, I know you can heal me, you can raise me up!" But nothing happened. The depression was relentless. The depression went on for so long that he began begging God to take it all away, bargaining with God that he would do whatever it took to rid himself of this life of lingering quiet desperation. Then one day, while kneeling in prayer, God spoke. The voice was not audible but was nonetheless clear. "There is something I need to do in you and through you and the only way I can do it is through this illness and conflict. Stay the course. Trust me. I will accomplish my purposes in your life." From that moment on my fiend changed the tone and words of his prayers from, "Lord, heal me," to "Lord, don't heal me until you have accomplished all that you want to accomplish in me."

My friend said, "Jeff, the first time I prayed this prayer, I didn't really mean it. I just wanted out. I thought if I said the right words that maybe God would have mercy and rip this awful depression away from me. However, the more I began to pray this prayer, the more I realized that my life was about something bigger than my personal convenience. Then, and only then, did my attitude change." He related to me the reality that his prayers evolved into more patient, submissive requests and that within a few months the symptoms were gone and he felt renewed. Let's just get it out into the open. My friend has no idea to this day why God allowed this plague of depression. However, he assumes that someone close to him experienced a transformation while witnessing his response to it. Moreover, he firmly believes that without this unfortunate season of life he may never have come to know God the way God seeks to be known. Indeed, "Faith is confidence in what we hope for and assurance about what we do not see" (Hebrews 11:1).

✦ ✦ ✦ ✦ ✦ ✦ ✦ ✦ ✦

The culture shock of the Christian walk is that Jesus calls us to give it all, or don't give at all. You can't have it both ways. You can't straddle the fence. You can't focus on both the world and God. The beauty of the Christian walk is that sometimes the thing or the place that you think is the most dangerous or volatile often proves to be the safest place of all. That's where Jesus shows up! He hangs out in furnaces.

Shadrach, Meshach, and Abednego were just walking around in the fire, hanging out with God. They're not bound, they're not burnt, and they're just hanging out with Jesus. The trial that you are in will not last forever, as much as it feels like it might. That furnace is temporary. God will use the furnace to burn off whatever is binding you, but He does not send you into it alone. God walks with us through every furnace that we face. God is shaping and molding you and He is with you every step of the way, holding your hand the entire time.

Are you a fully devoted follower? Do you have the faith to say, "Here am I, send me"? I want to live my life for something that truly matters, beyond myself and my little kingdom. I want to live for Him and His kingdom, which is eternal. What you do under pressure reveals your true self. So when the pressures of life weigh you down and the "fiery furnace" looms, will you be able stand for your God?

I have a friend named Ajai Lall. People love hearing his stories because he is a man of God who stands up for what is right, even in the face of persecution and possible death. He is an evangelist in India and he has looked down the barrel of a gun, knowing if he says the wrong thing at the wrong time he will be killed. Yet he stands firm because he is a fully devoted follower of Christ. There's an entire generation of young people in America right now wanting to see that kind of authenticity. They want to know if there is anyone out there who really lives in a manner that corresponds with their truth claims.

I don't pretend to know the depths of the mind of God. I only know that which has been revealed through Scripture, the ultimate point of reference. I have few guarantees in this world. If life continues to show you that you are not in control, then chances are, you are not in control. By all means, do the right thing. Do what is good and acceptable before God. Know however that this does not guarantee that you will live a conflict-free life. You and I have been bought with a price. God owns us, truly owns us. And while He is faithful and good, He also reserves the right to use us however He sees fit for His ultimate purposes in this world. Let's get it out in the open. God is doing something grandiose in this world and He is doing something very special in each one of us. He is engaging us in The Divine Romance! A romance that is so much deeper and lasts so much longer than anything this world has to offer, and, a relationship that is far more precious than the finest diamonds in the deepest caves of Africa.

CHAPTER 2

Making a Way for Love

Freewill is a powerful thing! To think that God created a world where each person possesses the power of decision is truly remarkable. One could argue that the world would have been a much better place had God simply removed the freewill mechanism and prohibited any choices not consistent with holiness and purity. What a world that would be! No crime, hate, murder, theft, jealousy, rape, cruelty, corruption or abuse of any kind. Sounds great, eh? Yes, if the purpose of creation was to create a little God cave where everything is highly controlled and immeasurably calculated. But what is the problem in such a scenario? There may not be any hate or violence but neither would there be love and loyalty. Love is a fragile thing. It requires freewill. You cannot have one without the other. Genuine love demands that such affection and devotion be given not out of fear or compulsion but out of a willingness of heart. Love that is forced is not love at all. You can force a person to do a lot of things but you cannot force them to love you. Love comes from deep down inside the soul. Love is not an involuntary response. Love is a choice you make. When someone says, "I love you," if the realistic option to say, "I don't love you," does not exist, then, this is not an expression of authentic love.

The Bible reminds us that we love God because He first loved us. God did something that drew us in and inspired our love and devotion. He spoke to us in the most powerful love language known to humanity. He gave up what was most precious to Him in order to take possession of us. When you begin to see God as He really is, you will embrace this grace given to you by God and begin to live a life of love and appreciation for His provision. It will suddenly dawn on you that no matter what happens in this life, God has made you for another world.

On the last page of *The Chronicles of Narnia*, C.S. Lewis writes:

> "For us this is the end of all stories . . . . But for them it was only the beginning of the real story. All their life in this world . . . had only been the cover and the title page: now at last they were beginning Chapter One of the Great Story, which no one on earth has read, which goes on forever and in which every chapter is better than the one before."

God has solved our ultimate problem and answered life's most penetrating question: What happens when we die? Jesus conquered death, therefore, so shall those who place their faith and trust in God. When you know how the story ends, you can endure the troubles and turmoil along the way. We will speak more of this later but for now it is important to remember that God has loved us from the beginning in hopes that we would use our freedom to respond to His love and draw near to Him. This explains so much about the world in which we live. Love and evil are two sides of the same coin. Love opens the door to evil in the sense that both require freewill. Once the freewill door is open, both evil and love can step in. Each individual chooses his companion. If God removes freedom then evil would surely dissipate, but, so would the potential for love. And since God created this world for love, He seems resigned to allow evil to exist for a season before completely eradicating it, but eradicate it He will.

In the meantime, He promises something that is quite miraculous. His promise is revealed in a verse popular among Christians but seldom fully considered by the same. He says, "I will work everything together for my good" (Romans 8:28). God is communicating to us that although He will allow evil to exist for a season in order to protect the integrity of love and freewill, He will take even the most heinous thing we could ever imagine and work it all together to accomplish His purpose of redemption on planet earth. That is indeed a remarkable statement. Yes, God could create a robotic type universe which would be miraculous indeed, but, He chooses to go one better. He is actually going to allow every person who has ever existed or will exist to use his/her freedom to pursue God or reject Him. For those who choose to draw near to God, he will use every event in their lives to accomplish His goal of Divine Romance and relationship. For those who reject Him, He will still use their most dastardly deeds to accomplish His purposes in the world. Think of it. It is one thing for a King to govern his kingdom by fear, intimidation and control. It is another thing altogether for a King to allow his subjects freewill and yet still achieve his desired end. Only one who stands outside time and space and is not limited to it could accomplish such a feat. That is God!

So, given the reality of our freedom to pursue or reject God, He begins His pursuit while we are young. His pursuits are both general and specific. Generally speaking, Paul in Romans 1 declared, "For since the creation of the world God's invisible qualities—his eternal power and divine nature—have been clearly seen, being understood from what has been made, so that people are without excuse" (Romans 1:20). When one considers the vastness of this universe and the created order in which we live, Paul says categorically that the evidence is clear. God exists and all men are without excuse. I must admit, I have spent a lot of time debating and conversing with Atheists and I find them to be a most peculiar people. (I'm confident they would say the same thing about me.) Although pleasant and enjoyable in their conversations, most Atheists possess a closed pre-commitment to Atheism. I do not want to move too far down the road of apologetics here. I have done that in other books, most deliberately in *Dinner With Skeptics*. But for our purposes here we must confess that the idea that any educated or uneducated mind could adhere to the theory of "something" emerging out of "total and complete nothingness" seems ludicrous if not imbecilic. Only a mind that fears the ramifications of a purposeful universe would come to such a conclusion. That is basically Paul's statement. He goes on to say that the problem with disbelief in God is not a lack of evidence but the suppression of it. This of course explains why children at a very young age live with the assumption that God exists. They enter the world in the early stages of divine courtship. Think for a moment. How far back does your knowledge of God go? Isn't it true that you really did not need your parents to tell you God is real? They may have taken you to church or helped you understand things about God, but, the reality of God's existence was a given almost from the time you could collectively put your thoughts together. When we are young the sense of wonder and amazement overwhelms us. Everything from food to physical touch to warm bath water to the sun, moon, and stars communicates a sense of beyond in us that catalyzes questions that we will be asking for the better part of our lives. Who made all of this? From where did we come? Toward what are we moving? All this is part of the general revelation that prompts the question of the meaning and purpose of our existence. The Psalmist tells us that the handiwork of God is a testimony to His creative capacity and love. These are the things that are supposed to draw us in to the courtship phase of our intimacy with God. If we seek God and search for Him with all of our hearts, we will find Him. God is forever and always closer than we ever imagined.

However, as powerful a communicator of the workings and doings of God that the Created order is, it is still merely general revelation. God goes far beyond that into what we call special revelation. This is God's specific work in an individual's life which is designed to draw him/her into a deeper intimacy and relationship. Yes, such evidence can be described as subjective but when coupled together with the objective evidence of God's general revelation, these experiences are powerful exhibits of God's desire to draw us in.

One such example of these subjective types of experiences occurred when I was twenty years old. As weird and odd as it was, it was truly a life-defining moment. Having been rejected by the division one school of which I had dreamed of receiving a basketball scholarship, that year was a particularly difficult year. Working three jobs and attending every try-out basketball camp under the sun, energy was low and countenance even lower. One afternoon I was working at Watson's Department Store in the men's clothing section when the manager of the store paged me to the front office ordering me to assist the air-conditioner repairman to the roof. The repairman fit every stereotype I had ever imagined. He had a rather obtrusive pot belly hanging over his belt and his drooping pants revealed things I would have rather not seen. His tool belt hung far below his waste and the smell of beer and hot dogs made me feel I was at the local carnival about to ride the Ferris wheel. At any rate, I followed him up the ladder to the top of the building toward the air-conditioning units hoping the scheduled maintenance would occur posthaste! With the July sun beating down on our heads "Bob the Builder" remained completely silent during the entire process, pausing from his work only for a moment to grunt toward the tools he expected me to place in his hands. Truly this was a man of deep thought and complex personality. Finally, after forty-five minutes of brutal heat and awkward silence, Yoda put down his tools, looked me straight in the eyes and said, "Son, have you ever stopped to think that perhaps God does not want you playing basketball but instead has something much better for you? You can't run from God forever young man." Expecting no rebuttal, Master Bob went back to work and spoke not another word for the duration of the tenuous repair job. I am not sure why his words had such an impact on me. I have no idea why a man who knew nothing about me could be so keenly aware of my personal struggles. I can't really explain much of what happened up there on that roof. In fact, I tend to be skeptical of experiences like that. Maybe Bob had simply had too many beers the night before. Still, something uncanny had occurred and I had no logical explanation for it. Subjective experiences can seldom be trusted. However, when experiences like this continue to occur over a period or season of life, we tend to stand up and take notice. This is merely one of the dozens of special revelations God gave to me along the way toward the path He had marked out for me. And not all the roads were easy. In fact, some were so difficult that I began to question whether or not God even existed. I'll talk about one very specific traumatic event in Chapter 9. Now, at fifty years of age, I am able to look back and see how God revealed Himself numerous times through specific events that at the time seemed meaningless or even unfortunate. Each of these events served as a link in the chain toward a more complete understanding of who God really is and the inner peace, contentment and even centralized joy that comes from knowing Him. In short my relationship with God is not that much different than my relationship with my wife.

WOOING MY WIFE

These two ideas of general and specific revelation are not difficult to understand. Every relationship experiences both. When I first met my wife Robin at Johnson University, I possessed a general understanding of who she was. I saw her in the breakfast line for the first time and thought, "Wow, this is the most beautiful woman I have ever seen!" I asked my friends about her. I learned certain things about her that were widely known. In other words, I was gathering general revelation. Robin, although born in Bedford, Indiana was raised in Zambia, Africa. She is the daughter of missionary parents who had given birth to two daughters of which Robin was the youngest. I learned that Robin loved the song, "Africa" by Toto and enjoyed dancing, hiking, and something called "Turkish Delight" with which I was unfamiliar at the time. I was glad to discover later that it had nothing to do with Turkish men. Other than these few facts, Robin seemed to be a rather closed book. Not much else was known. She had dated a few guys but nothing serious. She often spoke of returning to Africa but no one knew exactly why or for what purpose. And when I met her the only man in her life was Magnum, the name she had given her 1978 Mustang. One thing was certain, however, I wanted to "know" more.

I began pursuing her with a passion for knowledge and understanding. So, I took the first step by asking her out on a date. She said yes and the rest is history. The three years of dating that led to marriage were indeed some of the most frustrating and confusing years of my life. Courtship is a difficult phase. You often do not know where you really stand. In fact, Robin and I broke up three times during the courtship phase before we finally agreed to marry. The cause of the break-up was often associated with poor communication. We were two very different people. For those of you familiar with the emphasis placed on "Love Languages" in today's counseling, the next few lines will make perfect sense. For those unfamiliar, "Love Language" (Quality Time, Gifts of Affection, Physical Touch, Words of Affirmation, and Acts of Service) describes the five different ways in which one communicates and receives love. The significant aspect of this philosophy has to do with the manner in which one not only expresses love but the fashion in which they choose to receive or "feel" love as well. For instance, my love language is "Physical Touch" and "Words of Affirmation." When my wife touches me in an affectionate way or when she verbally expresses her love and appreciation for me, then, I hear the language of love and feel treasured and held in high regard. Herein lay the problem. Most men express the love language applicable to them without asking or considering the fact that the language that speaks love to you is not necessarily the language that speaks love to your wife. Robin's love languages are "Quality Time" and "Acts of Service." Imagine a lifetime of marriage where I attempt to communicate my love to my wife through "Words of Affirmation" and "Physical Touch" assuming that her love language is identical to mine. Although unintentional, I would be denying my wife the language of love for which she so desperately yearns. This is ignorance not selfishness.

During the dating phase of our relationship both Robin and I committed fundamental errors in regard to love languages. She seldom gave me "words of affirmation" and I hardly ever gave her "Quality Time." Now that is not to say that we did not spend time together. But hanging out watching basketball or football or going to movies is not Robin's (or any other woman's) definition of quality time. She needed to know that I genuinely longed to spend quality time together. I needed to hear her speak words of affirmation and affection. What each needed was seldom given. This is a recipe for disaster. Consequently, our relationship became marred by suspicion, doubt, fear, and ultimately frustration. We were certain that God had brought us together. We were sure about our feelings for one another. But our inability to speak the language of love to each other continued to endanger our survival. How we made it to the marriage altar I will never know.

The first seven years of marriage were both good and bad. We loved each other and were committed to this relationship. But we had not yet dealt with our "love language" issues and were drifting farther and farther apart. Robin was becoming more and more frustrated with the lack of quality time and I was becoming more and more frustrated with the lack of affirmation and physical touch. Like most newly married couples, we just didn't have a clue. Then one day, after a long day at work, I came into the bedroom to find Robin on the bed weeping. We had waited far too long. She felt unloved and was considering leaving and going back to live with her parents. I assured her that I loved her very much and that we should not give up. We sat and talked for a while, the first "quality time" we had had in months. Thank God we came to the conclusion that we needed counseling. I was "all in" and could not believe that I had let things get this far out of hand. I had become so concerned about climbing the ladder of success that I had completely abandoned my wife spiritually and emotionally. My relationship with Robin was disintegrating and it was time to act!

It was there in New Zealand where we experienced an incredible breakthrough. The "Love Languages" concept made perfect sense to me. Suddenly, it dawned on me that I had failed miserably to communicate love to my wife in a language that she understood and was beneficial to her. Discovering that her love languages were "acts of service" and "quality time" was like a light bulb going off in my head. The idea that the best way I could express my love to my wife was "to do the dishes" or "run the vacuum" had previously never crossed my mind. But now, with this new information, I could speak powerful words of affection through the simplest of activities. Moreover, I noticed that the more I engaged in her love language the more she engaged in mine. "Acts of Service" often led to "Physical Touch." "Quality Time" often led to "Words of Affirmation." These new discoveries led to greater longing for each other.

I learned a valuable lesson about relationships in the middle of all this. If we truly want to know someone intimately, we must make the commitment to go on a journey that is sure to be taxing, trying, and downright treacherous. Therefore, for any relationship to arrive at the desired destination, there must be a pre-commitment to weather inevitable storms. At any point we become uncommitted, the relationship begins to flounder on the waves of self-preservation and it's only a matter of time before the waves come crashing in.

This is precisely why the Bible speaks so much about covenants or agreements between two parties. Relationships are hard. Why? Two flawed people come together in the hopes of making one bliss-filled, joy-filled relationship. Yea, right. How does that math work? Unless we enter relationships with a pre-commitment to longevity, the odds of remaining together are slim to none. Flawed people are just that—flawed, self-centered, self-aggrandizing, and self-promoting. Relationships require a promise to make every attempt to care as much about the other person as you do yourself and to fight hard to conquer every storm that comes your way. Otherwise, the relationship will never last.

This is where we come to an important juncture of this book. I don't think most of us realize how committed God is to revealing Himself to us in a way that communicates the depths of His love and His commitment to do whatever it takes to enter into intimacy with Him. Again, yes, we have been saved by grace through faith in Jesus' work on the cross. I get that. I am confident you do as well. But this is merely the door that opens up to us the possibility of knowing God as He seeks to be known. In fact, and here is the rub, even if we are not passionate about pursuing an understanding and knowledge of God through the spiritual disciplines of prayer, worship, and Scripture, God never gives up His commitment to reveal Himself to us in a way that creates an appetite for more. In fact, the more we engage in prayer, worship, and Bible reading, the less aggressive God needs to be in our everyday lives. The less involved we are in seeking God, the more involved He must become in doing whatever it takes to get us back on path.

Did you hear about the guy who wanted to do something special for his mother's eightieth birthday? He sent her two very special birds, Parrots, that were able to sing, dance, and talk. These birds cost five thousand dollars each. Anxious to discover his mother's reaction, the son phoned his mother a week after her big day and asked, "How did you like my gift?" Her response? "O son, they were very tasty. I enjoyed them very much." Shocked, the young man exclaimed, "Mom, those were very special birds! They were very expensive. You were not supposed to eat them! They can sing, dance, and talk!" To which his mother quipped, "Well, they should have said something."

Another pastor friend of mine in Savannah, Georgia told me that a middle aged woman who had lived a rather disastrous life came to his church one weekend and within a few short months gave her life to Jesus and jumped right into Bible study and service projects. Then suddenly, without warning of any kind, she disappeared.

He phoned her one weekend and asked if everything was okay. She responded honestly by saying that she was actually experiencing buyer's remorse. When asked to elaborate she responded, "Well, I gave my life to Jesus and nothing has changed. I still have the same old problems, same old debt, and same old relationship issues. Somebody should have said something!" Maybe she is right. Maybe we need to stop pretending that when you come to Jesus your life actually gets easier and all your problems are solved. Maybe we need to speak the truth that while some of your problems may dissipate, others actually intensify under the weight of an unbelieving world. Moreover, we need to consider that perhaps God Himself is responsible for the increased tension in your life. His sole purpose is to expose and destroy anything that stands in the way of perfect intimacy between you and Him. Sometimes He just has to squeeze you until all the infection is removed and the healing can begin.

Make no mistake, God wants relationship with us and not merely a functional relationship but one that goes deep into our very mind, heart and soul. As intensely desperate as we are to know God, He is even more determined to reveal Himself to us. Until we know God as He seeks to be known we will never experience the abundant life Jesus came to bring. Therefore, motivated out of love, God does what He has to do to give us the best chance of knowing Him in a way that transforms everything about us and grants us the peace and joy that passes anyone's understanding, sometimes even our own.

Before we center into what I believe is God's primary method of revelation, we need to be reminded of the covenant He has made with us extending all the way back to Abraham and all the way through to the Day of the Lord when Christ returns. This covenant is perhaps the most crucial aspect about your relationship with God and your ability to begin the process of knowing who God really is. We can speak in general terms about God but if we desire to experience Him on a very deep and intimate level, we must begin here, with Abraham, and his experience with God in Genesis 15.

Abraham had four dramatic encounters with God. In Genesis 12 God told Abraham to get out from his people, get out from his land, get out from his family, and, get out from his country." Leave your father's house and everything that is familiar to you and go to a land that I will show you. Abraham's response to this daunting challenge? "So Abraham got out not knowing wither he was going." Imagine packing everything up, leaving town with all your family and possessions, having no real clue concerning the destination. The second visit occurs in Genesis 15. This time God proclaims to Abraham that He will become a great nation with offspring that will become as numerous as the stars in the sky and the sand on the seashore, and, One of those offspring will bless the entire world! Abraham would have the right to assume a few things at this point. He could count on the fact that, one, a child would be given to his wife Sara, and, two, that God would generously give him a new protected territory in which his descendants could live and flourish.

Unfortunately, by the time we arrive in chapter fifteen, years have passed and Abraham is beginning to wonder if any of this will actually happen. In fact, it is here is Genesis 15 that Abraham questions God concerning both the land and the child. Then, as we make our way toward Genesis 17, Abraham is chomping at the bit wondering what in the world is going on with God. Abraham reminds God of His promises and exclaims, "Lord, you said you were going to give me a son, and, well, we have been waiting 25 years. I am 99 years old and my wife Sara is 90. What gives?" (My paraphrase of course). How does God reinforce His promises in the face of Abraham's skepticism? God simply says, "Just wait!"

Before we move on lets make a quick application. How true it is that we can never really know the miraculous power of God until He places us into a situation where the only possible way forward is through miraculous intervention. As long as we are able to make our own way, we don't really need God nor will we seek to discover what God is actually capable of. To know God and the power of His might, we must be placed into a situation where the only thing that can save us is God Himself. If there is any other way out, we will take it! Moreover, we will not give God the glory when the victory comes. It is just the way we are. Therefore, if God wants us to truly know what He is capable of, then, He must put us into a situation where the rug is pulled out from under us and the only way forward is through divine intervention. Then we will know that God is able to do immeasurably more than we could ever ask or imagine.

Finally, in Genesis 22, Isaac is born. The long awaited promise has become reality. Just as Abraham and Sarah are celebrating the boyhood years of a beloved son, God speaks to Abraham again. God says, "Abraham, take your son, your only son, the one you love with all your heart, to the top of the mountain and sacrifice him on the altar there to me." Wow! What kind of God is this? Why would He require such a thing? Before we take a closer look at the answer to that question, consider a review of Abraham's life.

First, God tells Abraham to leave his land. Abraham says, "Where am I going?" God responds, "I will show you later. Just go!" Then, God says to Abraham, "I will give you a land." Abraham says, "Where is this land?" God says, "I will tell you later. Just wander!" Thirdly, God says to Abraham, "I will give you a child." Abraham responds, "When?" God says, "I will tell you later. Just wait." Finally, God commands Abraham, "Sacrifice your child." Abraham says, "Why?" God says, "Tell you later. Just walk up the mountain! Take the knife and the fire."

The manner in which God worked in Abraham's life is not the exception but the rule. These are very difficult circumstances in which God placed Abraham with very little knowledge of the strategic details concerning each situation and how they would in fact be fulfilled. Each step along the way is going to require patience and faith on Abraham's part. Yet, each step of the way will inspire Abraham to seek and know God in a way he had not previously experienced. Abraham is growing in his knowledge of God because God is revealing Himself through extremely difficult circumstances that require Abraham to search and seek Him with all of his heart, soul, and mind.

This journey of a lifetime produced something very special in Abraham. A key verse in the Abraham narrative is Genesis 22:5 where Abraham, just before his ascent to the top of the mountain where he was told to sacrifice his son, looked to his servant and said, "Stay here with the donkey while I and the boy go over there. We will worship and then we will come back to you" (Gen. 22:5). Interesting. Abraham, even before making the journey with Isaac to the altar of sacrifice, knew that God would never have him actually go through with it. He knew that both he and the boy would "come back to you (the servant)." Abraham had learned enough about God to know that this was not the kind of God that would have a father sacrifice his own son. Then why have Abraham go through the ordeal. Although we can not know with absolute certainty, it seem tenable to assume that God was still removing the idols from Abraham's life.

If we truly desire to know God as He seeks to be known then we must pursue Him more than any other pursuit in our lives. The temptation is to place such a high value on something God has provided or has yet to provide that that thing or person becomes that which we give ultimate worth. But only God is supposed to sit in that chair. God requiring Abraham to march up the mountain was not so much a test for Abraham as it was an event of confirmation for Abraham. The moment Abraham was willing to drop the knife on his own son was precisely the moment Isaac ceased to be

Abraham's idol. Abraham's ultimate pursuit and allegiance toward God maintained their integrity and by being willing to lose one Abraham gained both. But all of this had been settled long before Abraham began the journey up the mountain. Although Abraham had grown so much in his knowledge and understanding of God, he still needed a practical experience to reinforce the goodness and faithfulness of God. He received both from his mountain top excursion.

Again, this is simply the fashion in which God operates. Knowing Him is a life long journey that pays huge dividends along the way. The problem is that when the rug is pulled out from under us we seldom see the experience as God extending His hand to take us into deeper intimacy and fellowship with Him, as well as a deeper understanding of who He truly is and what He can actually do in us. For most of us, we see difficult circumstances as God's abandonment. So, we run from God rather than to Him when the bottom drops out from beneath us.

Now, the beauty of all this is that God desperately desires to build staying power in us. Because He wants to reveal Himself even more than we want to know Him, He wants to help us get the anchor down deep into the waters so that we can hold steady and true during the most difficult storms, some of which, are a direct result of His drawing us into a deeper relationship. Deep waters do not always result in deep people. More often than we would like to admit, deep waters catalyze anger, bitterness, and rage. The reason for this is that our primary pursuit is still not God. We would much rather create God in our own image rather than allow Him to shape us into His. Again, however, God knows our tendency, so, beginning with Abraham, God wants to help us get the anchor down. How did He accomplish this with Abraham? Before God began placing Abraham into difficult situations, He first established an unbreakable covenant with him.

The writer of the book of Hebrews understood the significance of the events of Genesis 15 very well. He writes: "Because God wanted to make the unchanging nature of his purpose very clear to the heirs of what was promised, he confirmed it with an oath. God did this so that, by two unchangeable things in which it is impossible for God to lie, we who have fled to take hold of the hope offered to us may be greatly encouraged. We have this hope as an anchor for the soul, firm and secure" (Hebrews 6:17-19).

The writer is referring to the covenant ratification ceremony that took place between God and Abraham in Genesis 15:

"So the Lord said to him, 'Bring me a heifer, a goat and a ram, each three years old, along with a dove and a young pigeon.'

¹⁰Abram brought all these to him, cut them in two and arranged the halves opposite each other; the birds, however, he did not cut in half. ¹¹Then birds of prey came down on the carcasses, but Abram drove them away" (Genesis 15:9-11).

What on earth is happening here? This seems quite bizarre! At least to you and me. Abraham, however, knew exactly what God was doing. To help us understand, let's bring this idea into present reality. When most of us enter into a contract with someone else, there are promises made and signatures applied. In New Zealand, the two parties involved in the marriage contract will actually sign their names as part of the official ceremony. As someone sings a song of love, the bride and groom will kneel down before a beautifully decorated table and with golden pen signify their promises to each other. Here in America we do similar things, especially when purchasing any kind of property.

For instance, my wife Robin and I recently bought a house in California. When we arrived at the real estate agency, we could hardly believe the amount of documentation requiring both our signatures. Page after page demanding we solidify our promises with a signature. The entire contract was about our promise to pay. Every signature reminded us of the covenant we were making with the bank. The signatures answer the banks questions: How can we know you will pay us back? How can we be certain that you will keep your word? If there is no signature, there is no requirement or expectation or consequences. However, if you sign, you are bound by the signature that seals the covenant you've made.

However, Abraham did not live in a written culture but an oral storytelling one. No pens, papers or signatures required, or, available for that matter. When two entities entered into a contract with each other, as a sign of their promises to each other, each member would act out the consequences of his/her unfaithfulness publicly, in front of everyone else. So, rather than sign a contract, people in Abraham's day would bring different kinds of animals, cut them into two separate pieces, lay one half of the animal on one side and the other half on the other side and then purposefully walk between the pieces. This act communicated to all witnesses that you were making a public declaration that if you did not uphold your end of the contract and accomplish everything you were promising to accomplish, then, may what happened to these animals happen to you! You were publicly declaring, "If I don't do everything I have promised to do, may I be cut off from the land of the living. May I be utterly destroyed. May my flesh lay on the ground to feed the birds of the air and the beasts of the field." You were in fact acting out the curse, saying, "May God bring destruction on me if I fail to keep my promise."

When Abraham was told to bring the animals and cut them into pieces, he would have known what God was doing. This was a covenant ratification ceremony. He must have been elated. "God is entering into a public commitment with me." "God is going to solidify His promise." But there is no way he could have anticipated what happened next.

> As the sun was setting, Abram fell into a deep sleep, and a thick and dreadful darkness came over him. When the sun had set and darkness had fallen, a smoking fire-pot with a blazing torch appeared and passed between the pieces.

This is truly an amazing scene. The blazing torch and the smoking pot represent the glory of God. These are the same symbols used when God came down to Mt. Sinai to give Moses the Ten Commandments. Likewise, these symbols were familiar to those who had witnessed the presence of God during the exodus in the form of a pillar of cloud and fire. These are symbols of the Shekinah glory and overwhelming presence of the Omnipotent God. However, it was not only the awesomeness of God's presence that overwhelmed Abraham. Imagine Abraham's astonishment when the presence of God walked between the pieces! It's as if God were saying to Abraham, "Abraham, are you concerned that I will not fulfill all my promises to you?" "Are you questioning my commitment, love, and provision?" "Do you not yet know Me?" "Are you unfamiliar with my ways?" "Then I will walk between the pieces." And notice, God never requires Abraham to walk between the pieces as well.

Historically speaking, when a king entered into a covenant relationship with a servant, one of two possible scenarios occurred. Either both the servant and the king walked between the pieces or, the servant walked alone. Never would the king walk alone. It was the servant's honor that came under scrutiny, never the King's. God is doing something with Abraham that would change Abraham's view of God in a powerful and dramatic way. God is saying to Abraham, "Abraham, I am going to go through the pieces for both of us." "I know you will break your covenant with me but nevertheless I will keep my covenant with you." "I will take on the consequences for both of us!" This is astounding. God, in walking through the pieces makes a public declaration, "Abraham, may I be cut off from the land of the living if I don't keep my promises to you." Imagine. He who is immortal promises to become mortal. He who is immutable promises to suffer mutation. He who is responsible for all life promises to be cut off from the living, suffer finitude, bruised, torn, pierced and destroyed, if, He fails to keep His covenant with Abraham.

Now, if the narrative ended here, the story would certainly be almost too fantastical to believe. But God reveals something about Himself that Abraham would have never anticipated or known had God not chosen to reveal it to him. By walking through the pieces alone, God delivers the Good News of the Gospel long before Jesus is ever born.

Lets face it. For most of us, if we really think about our relationship with God, it's not so much about our doubting God's ability and willingness to keep His promises. No, rather, the issue that concerns us is that somehow, we will violate the covenant we have made with God, thus, forfeiting our right to receive the promised blessings. This is the beauty of this narrative. When God walks alone through the pieces, He is proclaiming, "Abraham, I know human nature. I know although you may passionately pursue faithfulness concerning our agreement, there will be times when you will break the promises you have made. But Abraham, let me help you discover something about Me that you would have never known except I reveal it to you. Abraham, may I be cut off if I don't do my part of the bargain, but Abraham, may I be cut off if you don't do yours."

This is beyond anything Abraham would have anticipated. God's heart for Abraham is so intensely filled with love and acceptance that He gives the assurance, "I am going to bless you Abraham even if it means that I will have to die!" "Abraham, may I be cut off from the land of the living if you or I break this covenant between us." What happened centuries later? Darkness came down again. "At noon, darkness came over the whole land until three in the afternoon. And at three in the afternoon Jesus cried out in a loud voice, 'My God, my God, why have you forsaken me?'" (Mark 15:33-34). Jesus, the God-man, was cut off from the land of the living. The impossible became possible. Immortality became mortality. Immutability suffered mutation. Jesus was bruised, torn, pierced and destroyed. He was cut off from the land of the living temporarily that we might live at home with the Father for all eternity. Isaiah knew this day was coming when he recorded the prophecy:

> For he was cut off from the land of the living;
> for the transgression of my people he was punished.
> He was assigned a grave with the wicked. . .

> though he had done no violence,
>   nor was any deceit in his mouth.
> Yet it was the Lord's will to crush him and cause him to
> suffer, and though the Lord makes his life an offering for
> sin, he will see his offspring and prolong his days,
>   and the will of the Lord will prosper in his hand.
>
> Is. 53:9-10

Here is the point of all of this. Our relationship with God is divine, or, the Divine Romance. When we call on the name of Jesus we do so because we have realized that there is a gap between us and God due to our transgressions. God has "walked between the pieces" for us so that nothing could separate us from His love and mercy. At that point, Jesus comes on the inside through the power and presence of the Holy Spirit to do two things. First, to teach us all things knowable about God. The divine courtship we will discover God with each new day as we commit to enter into fellowship with Him. Although we will often falter in our commitment, if we hope to truly know God, we will have to make the decision that even when failure to pursue God sets in from time to time, we must get back up on the horse and start riding again. Remember, God walked between the pieces. He is committed to entering into relationship and intimacy with us even during those seasons when we abandon Him for things of far less value. That's where the second aspect of God's work in us comes to the forefront. Jesus is committed to sweeping your life clean of any and all things that hinder the full knowledge of God becoming a reality in you.

As I write this chapter I am in Chiangmai, Thailand drinking an excellent Latte on the campus of Payap University where my daughter Sian is taking language lessons. I woke up this morning to read my favorite devotional, *Walking With God*, by Chris Tiegreen. I don't think I could illustrate this point any better than Chris, so, with permission, I record his words:

> As Jesus is overturning the money-changing tables in the Temple, He quotes Isaiah 56:7, a verse from a passage about Sabbath-keeping and God's worldwide mission—"a house of prayer for all nations," Isaiah reads (emphasis added). It is a striking irony: The money changers had a limited effect on who could worship God by their monetary controls and exploitation, while Jesus speaks of global inclusiveness of the true worship of

God. They had missed the whole point about worship—it is to be freely and joyfully given. God's house is about prayer. Nothing else. Not profit, not experience, just pure, undefiled communion with Him. The New Testament application of this is not what we might think. We often apply Jesus' indictment of the money changers at the Temple to our own church building. They, too, are to be houses of prayer, of course. But Jesus never calls a church building "God's house." Neither do any of the New Testament writers. God's house, after the gift of the Spirit, is the heart of the believer. He dwells in us—individually and corporately. And as His house, we are the house of prayer. John 21:17 tells us that Jesus is consumed by His zeal for His Father's house. Knowing that we are His father's house makes that verse profound indeed. Jesus will zealously pursue communion in you, even if it means overturning some tables! (emphasis mine).

—Chris Tiegreen, July 23rd

Get the point? God is committed to this relationship whether we are or not. Again, salvation comes by grace through faith. If we are to have any relationship whatsoever with God our sin problem has to be dealt with. It has! On the cross Jesus took our guilt and shame and paid the penalty our sins deserve. God made a promise to Abraham that He himself would be cut off from the living before He would allow us to be eternally separated from Him. Through the cross we have come near to God. And now that God lives in us, some major sweeping and table turning will occur. This is the only way for us to know God as He seeks to be known. The problem, as we will see in the coming chapters, is that when God turns the tables over or begins to sweep our spiritual house clean, we mistake God's action for abandonment, pushing ,us farther away, rather than the reality that God is bringing us even closer for a glimpse of His glory.

CHAPTER 3

We're All Runners!

The story is told of a little two-year-old boy named Frankie. One day, his mother watched from a distance as Frankie painstakingly dragged a kitchen chair over to the window of the living room. He paused for a moment to catch his breath before dramatically pulling back the curtains, climbing on to the seat of the chair, just standing before the opened window taking it all in like a young boy noticing a beautiful young girl for the first time. Mesmerized by it all, he allowed his mind to wander. Finally, with a heavy sigh of pleading he uttered, "Frankie, you've got to get out of here." If there is one phrase that summarizes humanity it's this: "I gotta get outta here!" The grass is greener on the other side of the fence. The view from over there must be better than the view from over here. The greatest experiences are the ones we have not yet had. No matter how good we have it now, in the present, we live with the constant sense of discontent. We are runners! Especially in today's world where so much is available at our finger tips. Long gone are the days of endurance. If something is not to our liking, we simply move onto the next thing. So most, not all, of our relationships tend to disintegrate over time. Unless we are in for the long haul, the struggles and challenges of living and being together become too difficult for many and the option to move to the other side of the fence in search of greener grass is too strong. In fact, it is truly remarkable how far we have come in the last 50 years.

The average family income is at least 75,000 dollars more than it was fifty years ago. The average life expectancy has jumped some fifteen to seventeen years from 67 to 84. Moreover, due to advances in medicine and cosmology, 50 year olds look and feel like 35 year olds did fifty years ago. Think about it. We are twice as rich as our parents, far more healthy than our parents. And, we feel much better and live much longer than our parents did.

Yet, we are less happy than our parents! In fact, the rate of depression among Americans is 15-20% higher now than in the 1950's. Twenty percent of Americans describe themselves as very unhappy! Go figure. In the span of one single generation, the depression rate increased 20 percent. When something increases in a generation even ten percent, we call that an epidemic!" This makes no sense. We are better off monetarily, do not suffer from disease as badly, and, we have a greater sense of liberty and freedom because we have the means to travel and see the world, yet, there is epidemic in America. We have lost happiness and no one knows where to find it.

The loss of happiness has little to do with what we don't have and more to do with the feeling that although we have so much we might be missing something else. Its like the baby who fights sleep not because he does not believe that sleep will be an enjoyable experience but because he is afraid that if he enters into sleep he may miss something he may have enjoyed even more. We here in Southern California call this the Disney Land effect. Disney Land claims to be the "happiest place on earth." You move from one thrill to the next trying to get your next happiness fix. So you "soar over California" (my personal favorite ride) but before the ride is even finished you are wondering if you will have to stand in line too long at the next enjoyable experience. So, you rush around all day from one pleasurable experience to the next unable to truly and fully enjoy the experience at hand.

I remember reading an article years ago entitled: "Exposure to Beautiful Women is Ruining Our Lives." The article talked about a study that took an in depth look at the satisfactory levels of young married men and young college single men with girlfriends. At the beginning of the study, the single young men as well as the young married men were asked to rate their present level of satisfaction concerning their current wife or girl friend. Then, after three months, those conducting the study placed the young men, both married and single, into private viewing rooms showing them numerous non-pornographic photos of gorgeous women from television, movies, and magazines. After the viewing session, the hosts once again asked the young married and singles to rate their satisfaction level with their present spouse or girl friend. The satisfaction level decreased significantly! Why? The study revealed that before 1950 the average male might see five to ten beautiful women in his entire lifetime. But today, with the popularity of television and movies and easy access to both, a man can see nearly 200 beautiful women every night during three hours of television. In short, men are losing interest in their wives or girlfriend not because they feel their wife or girlfriend is unattractive or uninteresting. It goes much deeper than that. They now think they can do better! They now believe that they deserve better! A young man often finds it difficult to fully appreciate his present relationship because he believes he may be missing something even better.

The real problem with our lack of knowing and understanding the nature of God has nothing to do with God hiding from us and more to do with our unwillingness to forsake lesser things that we might gain that which is far greater. At some point in your life you must not only admit this tendency to run from God toward temporal unfulfilling endeavors, but, aggressively, passionately, and intentionally make the turn toward home. Jesus said, "You will find me when you seek me with all of your heart." What does that mean? It means that although there may be other loves in your life, God has to become your first and greatest love. Many God-fearing salvation experiencing people will possess a deep down desire to walk this road less traveled but will continually find themselves distracted by other less important things they think they might be missing. Others however, will fear the act of running toward God because they fear that doing so may expose the shallowness of their own pursuits and their lack of faith that knowing God is truly better than any other human experience. The point is, we all run from God to some degree. When this happens, God will often begin stripping us of everything we depend upon other than Himself. One by one He begins removing our idols, turning the tables, and sweeping the house clean. After all, God knows that we will never know Jesus is all we need until Jesus is all we have.

Jesus Himself categorically stated, "If anyone would come after Me, he must deny himself and take up his cross and follow Me. For whoever wants to save his life will lose it, but whoever loses his life for Me will find it. What good will it be for a man if he gains the whole world, yet forfeits his soul?" (See Matthew 16:24-26a). If I could take you to Corinth today I could show you the judgment seat where Paul was accused and tried for allegedly starting a riot. As the Roman judge lectured Paul concerning his Roman citizenship he would have reminded Paul of the oath he had assumed under the governing authorities. I can hear the judge say something like, "Paul, you are a Roman citizen and are responsible for taking up your cross daily for the cause of Rome. You have forfeited all your rights, goals, and dreams to Rome. You have a new master now. You can pursue other things but nothing greater or more intense than Rome. Do you understand this?" This is precisely why Jesus uses similar language in the context of full devotion to Him. Rome required your soul promising nothing in return. Jesus required your heart, soul and mind promising everything in return. In fact, Jesus promised that if you die to yourself and pursue God, you will gain everything. But, if you try to save your own soul in alternative pursuits, you will end up losing everything. "For whoever wants to save his life will lose it, but whoever loses his life for Me will find it." This is one of the most profound statements anywhere in literary antiquity. What did Jesus mean?

Like most little boys growing up in the south, I played Pee Wee baseball. My mom would wash and press my little red and white uniform and I would march out onto the field twice a week during the summer time to participate in America's favorite pastime. I loved playing the games but I hated the endless hours of shagging balls in the outfield during practice sessions. Furthermore, I played in left field. Left field is where they put you when you have no talent. Baseballs seldom travel to left field. No one in Pee Wee Baseball has the power to belt the ball that far. During these long practice sessions I would often daydream about all kinds of different things—ice cream, blue birds, chocolate etc.. However, my favorite past time activity included looking at the sun for about thirty seconds and then closing my eyes as tightly as I could to see the beautiful colored dots of red, green, purple, yellow and blue bouncing around under my eye lids. (Please don't try this at home. I am a professional Sun Watcher!). My only frustration was that the little dots were unstable, out of focus, bouncing to and fro. I yearned for the dots to move out of my peripheral vision into a more clear and captivating view. One day I learned the secret. When I gave up trying so hard to focus on the little dots and fixed my gaze at a defined point of reference in the background, then, and only then, would the little dots stabilize and come into focus in full viewing pleasure.

This is the message Jesus gives to His disciples. If you want to gain your life you must let it go. Stop focusing so hard on yourself and give your self and the little dots of your life to a more definitive point of reference, outside yourself, bigger than yourself, and suddenly, you will find that all the chaos of your life will stabilize causing the beauty of your life to come into a clear and enjoyable focus. If you truly want to find your way in this world, then stop focusing on the dots (your life) and fix your gaze on something bigger than yourself (God) and suddenly, all the chaos will settle and you will begin to see God and your life as they truly are. You gain your life by first letting it go. "A life devoted to things is a dead life, a stump: a God-shaped life is a flourishing tree" (Proverbs 11:28, *The Message*).

This should help us gain understanding into the words of Eric Henry Liddell, a Scottish athlete who won the Gold Medal in the Men's 400 meters at the Olympic Games of 1924 held in Paris, France. He said, "God has made me very fast and when I run I feel his pleasure!" However, winning the Gold Medal was not Liddell's primary objective. Long before pursuing the Gold Medal, Liddell determined that His greatest pursuit would be God Himself. By focusing his attention on God instead on his own self-aggrandizement, Liddell actually discovered both God and himself. In fact, I purposefully omitted the first part of Liddell's quote. He actually said, "God has made me for China, but, He has also made me very fast and when I run I feel His pleasure."

"God is most glorified when we are most satisfied in Him," says John Piper. There are fantastic by-products associated with searching and finding the God who wants to be found. However, these by-products come only when we seek Him above and beyond all other things. Once again, God is so passionate about us discovering Him in the way He seeks to be known that He is willing to strip everything away from us until we recognize the treasure that knowing Him really is. Sometimes, that means coming to the very end of ourselves.

I have often stated that if for some strange reason the only slice of the Bible you could access is Luke 15, you would still have the core message Jesus came to bring. It's the story of the prodigal son. Most of us know it. Remember? A father had two sons. The younger son, despite access to all the Father's wealth and resources, wanted to get out of the house, out from underneath his father's rule. Desiring to shake off the shackles, the son suggests something quite incredulous. Rather than waiting for his father to die and collect his inheritance, he asked his father for an advance. Although the western mind struggles with the concept, the eastern mind would have understood Jesus' point all too well. The young man was essentially saying to his father, "Dad, I wish to live as though you were dead." Jesus' audience would have been reeling in anger, astonished at the audacity of such a request. How dare the son of privilege scoff at the very one responsible for providing safety and security.

When Jesus told this story those who heard it were probably expecting the father to take his son out behind the woodshed and teach him some manners. Instead, the father in Jesus' story, took his savings, what would have sustained him in his old age, what he had for worked his entire life, and freely handed it over to his son. This is powerful and enlightening symbolism. If the Father represents God and the Son represents us, then the message is clear: when it comes right down to it, you and I have one of two options from which to choose in life: 1) We can choose to live at home with the Father or 2) We can live in a distant land far, far away from Him. That's the simplicity of life. Astounding is the reality that even though we know the good things that come with living at home with the Father, we still seem intent on journeying to a far away distant land. Why? Because we have never realized the true nature of the Father and the motivations of the restrictions He places upon us. We see them as boundaries that restrict freedom instead of parameters that bring life.

Most of my high school buddies believed in God. They also believed that there were advantages of living at home with the Father. However, the fact that the pursuit of God included respect for His precepts was simply too much to ask in their opinion. There was simply too much fun to be had away from the house out in the wilderness. This type of thinking only comes when the heart of the Father is not known or it's misunderstood. The irony is that although we feel restricted by the precepts of the Father, we still expect everyone else to live under them.

The young son in Jesus' story didn't want to live under the restrictions of his father because he failed to see them as motivated out of love. So, he gathered all he had and headed out to a distant country where he squandered his father's money in wild living. Can you imagine how the son must have felt as he was leaving? I'm free; I'm free at last! My father can't tell me what to do anymore. Off with the chains and the restrictions. Dad is not around to tell me what to do anymore and I am going away to live the high life! Inevitably it all feels good at first until your wrong actions rob you of your family, your marriage, your children, or your job. Ask anyone who has overcome or is still fighting an addiction. It may be thrilling at first but sooner or later it destroys you. Pornography is exciting, until you lose your job because your employer catches you. The affair is thrilling, until your wife discovers it and leaves you and your family is completely torn apart. Drugs are fun, until you do something stupid and they take your children from you. It all seems great at first until you find yourself undone and broken!

The point is that we are all runners. We run not because we do not want to know the Father but because we want to live apart from His restrictions. In fact, Christ-followers will tell you that when they first make a commitment to a regular prayer time, God often brings the sin in their lives to the surface so that they may first deal with them before moving on toward a greater intimacy. Yes, we are saved by grace through faith and have been given the gift of forgiveness. However, the sin that continues to entangle us may not rob us of our salvation but they do indeed short circuit or stifle our intimacy with God while stagnating our ability to know God as He wants to be known. The problem is not with God. It is with us. As soon as the conviction comes that we are not living appropriately in some area of life, we tend to run from God not toward Him. If conviction comes into our prayer life we tend to stop praying or we try to somehow block it all out of our minds while at the same time attempting to commune with God. You cannot live at home with the Father without dealing with the sins you are committing in a distant land. True repentance and confession are a huge part of progressing in our relationship with God and beginning to know and see God as He really is.

If you ever truly hope to know God as God seeks to be known, you must allow God to be God and His Word to be The Word that matters most in your life. This will only occur when you begin to see God as a Father who truly has your best interests in mind. Some of the urges and emotions with which you will have to struggle are a real and present danger that can only be overcome by the power of God and your own personal commitment to submit to God in every walk of life. It is not a matter of perfection but a matter of the will. The pursuit is what God is most concerned with. His grace covers a multitude of sin but not the multitude of willful disobediences and purposeful separations associated with a heart that is resistant to His love and precepts.

To make sure we understand this invaluable truth, lets place it into the context of something we are facing today. We are enamored with sex, money and power to the degree that they have become our idols. We want these things more than anything else—even more than the knowledge of God. In fact, we often use God in hopes that He will help us attain these things. How ironic. We often implore God to help us get our real saviors. "God, help me get the girl and I will serve you forever." "God help me get this promotion, house, raise, or beach house and I am yours." What an image of contradiction! Instead of God mattering most to us, we want God to help us get the things that matter most to us. If He fails to deliver we question His love or even His existence. Sex, money and power are our greatest pursuits and no one, including God, is going to keep us from them. Sex is the most powerful allurement of the three. We are possessed with it. It is everywhere. And once again, we will not allow God to draw the parameters because we have not yet comprehended His fences as the boundaries by which He protects us from ourselves. And, there is something else at stake.

In Exodus 3:12 Moses asks God for some sort of sign that He would be with him through the entire Exodus ordeal. Moses, lacking self-confidence and unsure that the people of Israel would submit to his leadership, begged God to give him a sort of written guarantee that things would work out well in the end. God's response is classic. He says, "I will be with you. And this will be the sign to you that it is I who have sent you: when you have brought the people out of Egypt, you will worship God on this mountain." What is God saying? He is reminding Moses that if it's feelings that Moses is after, or, if Moses needs to feel God's presence through this endeavor, then, the most effective way for that to happen is for Moses to obey God's commands. Its almost as if God says, "Moses, you want a guarantee that I will be with you? You will know with certainty that I was with you when you have completed the task for which I have called you and stand and worship me on the mountain for all that I have done." This is uncanny. In other words, if Moses wants certainty that God will be with him, then, he needs to obey God. We have lost our ability to "feel" God because we have lost our willingness to "obey" Him.

Obedience is a difficult thing for us and we severely underestimate the connection between obeying God and the feeling of experiencing Him. We are all runners. We run from God not because we do not want to know Him but because in knowing Him we begin to know ourselves and the sin that entangles us. Rather than allow God to do His work of redemption in us we would rather live in a distant land and take our chances away from the Father believing that He will receive us by His grace in the end. While this may be true, the reality is that we will never know the Father as He seeks to be known and the abundant life Jesus came to bring will never be ours to possess. In fact, many will destroy themselves before allowing Christ to dictate the type of lives they ought to live.

The response to the same-sex marriage issue reminds me once again that the issue is not really about same-sex marriage. This is merely symptomatic of something else. The real problem in all of this has to do with the battle between subjective and objective morality. One young lady, in response to my statement, wrote: *"I'm sorry but the God I know is a LOVING God and I just can't wrap my head around him not accepting someone into heaven for loving another person who happens to have the same "parts" as them...."* But wait! How does she know God is a loving God? Who told her? Maybe God is the big bad cosmic boss who wants to pound us into submission. In fact, how does she know anything about God? How does anyone know anything about God? Including me. Both she and I assume that God is a loving God. From where does such information originate? Who or what is the source? Is there any real proof for such an assumption? Or, have we merely created God in our own image? Have we said in our heart, "This is what God ought to be like, therefore, this is what God is like." These questions are at the core of this issue. Unless there is some kind of objective point of reference that reveals the character and nature of God, then what is said about God is nothing more than subjective and often self-preserving. Without an objective point of reference no definitive statement about God is possible. We may say that God is love, but we have no more standing than the person who claims that God is hate. So, does such an objective point of reference exist? Is there anything written or spoken about God that can help us distinguish between the ideal (what we want God to be) and the real (what God actually is). Jesus believed so. He believed that God revealed Himself to the world through the power of the written word. He said, "For truly I tell you, until heaven and earth disappear, not the smallest letter, not the least stroke of a pen, will by any means disappear from the Law until everything is accomplished" (Matthew 5: 18). And Jesus understood that He himself was the ultimate revelation of the Father. That's why He told His disciples, "If you have seen Me, you have seen the Father" (John 14:9). In other words, if you want to truly know what God is like, look at the Son and the words He has spoken.

These words not only refer to the words Jesus spoke during His three and a half years of public ministry but the words He has spoken throughout history. John 1:1-3 states, "In the beginning was the Word, the Word was with God and the Word was God. He was with God in the beginning. Through him all things were made; without Him nothing has been made." Then in John 1:14, "The Word became flesh and made His dwelling place among us." In other words, Christ is the author of both the spoken and written word. Christians hold this belief so dearly that, during times of conflict with culture, they often go back to the Bible in order to stand on the word of God no matter what the consequence. An overarching message found throughout the Bible tells us that, left to our own devices, we will create God in our own image. We will erect a God of convenience that just happens to like all the same things we like and disapprove of all the things we disapprove. The Bible constantly points us back to the reality of our tendency to suppress any truth that does not fit the utopia we think we can create apart from God.

The point is simple. The Christ-follower truly believes that God has revealed His will and purpose for mankind in the spoken and written words of the Bible. Furthermore, within the pages of Scripture are defined the parameters inside which man is to live his life for the good of man as a whole and for the good of the creation over which he rules. And here is the rub. You don't get to pick and choose. For the Christian, his/her opinions about God, or anything else for that matter, must align with the objective truth God has revealed about Himself. In fact, the young lady who said, "I'm sorry but the God I know is a LOVING God," does not realize that she has come to such a conclusion because she has grown up in a culture that has been heavily influence by the Christian world view. The problem is that she moves from the objective truth that God is love to a subjective opinion about how God's love should be demonstrated. Unfortunately, her subjective opinion is in direct conflict with the objective truth she claims exists. Logically, this just does not work.

If you are going to work from the objective point of reference that God is a loving God as revealed in the Bible, then other assumptions you make about God, morality, origin, meaning, purpose and destiny must also come from the same objective source. The question is not: What do I think God ought to be like?" Instead, the question is: "What is God truly like as revealed in the objective source?" Or, in the context of the lovely young lady who protested, *"I'm sorry but the God I know is a LOVING God and I just can't wrap my head around him not accepting someone into heaven for loving another person who happens to have the same "parts" as them...."* The real question is not, *"What do I believe God should think about sex between two men who have the same parts?"* Instead, her question should be, "What does God really believe about *sex between two men?"* Is there an objective source that can answer this question to any degree of certainty? Again, Christians would say, "Yes." The same Bible that tells us that God is love also tells us:

> *"Do not have sexual relations with a man as one does with a woman; that is detestable."*
>
> Lev. 18:22

> *"Or do you not know that wrongdoers will not inherit the kingdom of God? Do not be deceived: Neither the sexually immoral nor idolaters nor adulterers nor men who have sex with men nor*

thieves nor the greedy nor drunkards nor slanderers nor swindlers will inherit the kingdom of God."

1 Cor. 6:9-10

"They exchanged the truth about God for a lie, and worshiped and served created things rather than the Creator—who is forever praised. Amen. Because of this, God gave them over to shameful lusts. Even their women exchanged natural sexual relations for unnatural ones. In the same way the men also abandoned natural relations with women and were inflamed with lust for one another. Men committed shameful acts with other men, and received in themselves the due penalty for their error.

Romans 1:25-27

The problem is that we want to be the God of God and the Author of Scripture. God is a God who established marriage between a man and a woman whether we like it or not. The problem is that we are children who think we know better how the universe should operate, and, we do not trust that God truly has our best interests in mind. The fact that we take from the Bible what we like and discard what we detest speaks volumes about our generation. Nobody, including God Himself, is going to tell us what to do or how to live. We will live in the manner we see best. Our trust is in ourselves.

Unfortunately, everybody runs to some degree. The reasons may vary. We run because we believe that if we pursue God we may have to give up something precious. We run because we think that living at home with the Father is laborious and robs us of something greater we may experience in the distant land. The Prodigal Son is the story of you and me. And many of our stories do not end well. Jesus says, "After he had spent everything, there was a severe famine in that whole country, and he began to be in need" (Luke 15:14, *NIV*). So the son is tired, hungry, cold, and alone and he has one of two ways he can respond.

If you've never had knee surgery let me tell you a simple truth—it is very painful. A friend of mine had knee surgery; they actually drilled a few holes in his knee. When the doctor came in after the surgery my friend said, "So Doc, what's next?" The doctor calmly replied, "Pain, that's what's next!" He went on to explain. "There are two ways to deal with the pain. You can take a lot of pills to mask it, which only treats the symptoms, or you can face it head on and go to rehab." So he decided to go to rehab. The first therapist he worked with for the first few days was a very gentle, kind, empathetic woman with a soft touch, who showed great care and concern. She explained how to do simple exercises that only involved tiny, slow movements. If my friend showed any discomfort on his face she would just stop, make sure he was okay, and gently massage his knee. He summed up working with her this way: there wasn't much pain, but there wasn't much progress either. On the fourth day he moved on to his second therapist. She was a big, strong German woman. She moved him suddenly and quickly, stretching his knee and giving it stress every one to two minutes. His face was contorting in pain and he finally shouted, "I'm in pain, I'm in pain!"

Her response? "Yes, yes!" She said with alarming pleasure and enthusiasm. "Feel the pain, embrace the pain, and make it yours, the pain is your friend!"

Having recently broken both arms, I can sympathize with my friend. I have been looking so forward to this trip to Thailand. As the Pastor of a mega-church I often preach six times every weekend. I found this exhilarating at first but after seven years at this pace, I feel like every weekend takes a year off my life, which, if were true, I'd be dead by now, or, at least very old. At any rate, my biking accident occurred exactly three months before we were scheduled to depart LAX heading for Thailand. When the doctor told me that my left arm would be in a cast for six weeks, I began doing the math. I had never broken any bones before so at age 50 this was indeed a new, and painful, experience. Unaware that once the cast is removed weeks of rehab would follow until things returned to normality, I assumed I would be playing golf in plenty of time to enjoy the courses in Thailand. Imagine my rude awakening when the day they removed my cast they told me not to expect any aggressive activity for another three months. I was devastated! I was also determined. Immediately, I began seeing a massage therapist who loved inflicting pain and suffering. At just 5'2' tall, Terry was a little stick of dynamite. She sat, leaned, and elbowed her way up and down my arm, smiling a sadistic smile that seemed to experience great pleasure from my pain. There were times I wanted to sit up and smack her! When she periodically noticed my disdain she would say, "Do you want to play golf in Thailand or not?" Well, here I am in Thailand, just twelve weeks after my accident, writing this chapter on Thursday morning July 23rd after playing 36 holes of golf on Monday and Wednesday.

Do you see the analogy? Pain is often your friend to restore life and vitality. God is the compassionate Father who really loves you and desperately wants you to live at home with Him in His presence. Where there is God there is every good thing. Think about it! If God truly loves us and wants to give us the very best of everything, how far should He be willing to go to make sure we don't get sucked into the vortex of a world that settles for less valuable and temporal things?

My daughter Sian wanted a fish tank so we got one. The entire family left town one weekend and I was responsible for the fish. To those little fish, I was God. I determined whether they lived or died, whether it was light or dark, whether they were fed or starved. I gave those little fish everything, yet I didn't sense any gratitude. In fact, one of the little fish seemed to have an infected eye. The other fish kept trying to eat the dead flesh. This seemed to be killing the little fish so I removed him from the bowl to save his life. This proved far more difficult than I had imagined. It appeared as though the little fish thought I was trying to kill him. I had to chase that fish all over the bowl with his eyes bugging out and his little heart racing. I just knew I was going to give that little guy a heart attack! How I wished at that moment that I spoke "Fish."

Now, if the difference between my fish and me is great, how much greater is the difference between God and me? There might be something happening in your life right now that you see as God punishing you, when he's actually trying to save you. You see His hand coming down to squash you, when in reality He's trying to pull you out of something even worse than the pain you're in now. Maybe it's a relationship ended, a job lost, or an endeavor fell through, and you think God hates you but a loving God will do whatever it takes in your life, even inflict a bit of pain, to get to you turn your heart back to Him and come back home to the Father.

And God knows exactly where your breaking point is. It's not God's fault that most of us are so hard headed that it takes a long time before we get it. God removes things from our lives so that we finally reach a point where we come to the end of ourselves and realize that the things we have at home with the Father are priceless and incomparable to the things we find in the distant land. This is exactly what happens with the son as he comes to the end of himself. Lost, alone, and desperate, he hires himself out to a citizen of a foreign land who assigns him to the pigs. In Jesus' story we learn that the son longed to fill his stomach with the pods that the pigs were eating but no one gave him anything. It's important to note that in the culture of the first century if you wanted to tell someone to go away but you wanted to do it politely you offered them a job that you knew they wouldn't take. In this case, there's no way a young Jewish boy would take a job feeding pigs—no stinking way! Moreover, one can't make enough money to survive just by feeding pigs, so the young man was hoping to become an embezzler—an embezzler of pig pods. Instead of feeding the pods to pigs he was going to eat them himself.

When he finally comes to his senses the young rebel begins making good decisions. His eyes are opened to the futility and despair of the distant land and wisely decides it would be better to return home and ask to be a slave in his father's house than to live in a world that promises everything and delivers nothing. So, just as abruptly as he left the father's house, he now embarks on the journey home.

Have you ever opened your mouth and said something really dumb and then had to come back the next day and try to fix it? It's like a man who won the lottery one day and told his boss off the next. Imagine how he felt the third day when he discovered that hundreds of other people had also won the same lottery and his total winnings amounted to three hundred dollars. Ouch! Do you think he got his job back? We've all made mistakes from which it appeared impossible to recover. Just a few years ago I bought my wife what I believed at the time to be the perfect Christmas present. I had listened to her complain about her weight for over six months (she only weighs 125 pounds) and finally decided that I would get her the perfect gift. So, I ordered Nutri-system for her because I knew she would never do it for herself. Well, that's just about the dumbest thing a husband could ever do. I don't really know what I was thinking and quite frankly, by the time I realized my mistake, the Nutri-system boxes were at the front door. No matter how many times I apologized I simply could not recover.

With that personal illustration in mind, what do you think this young man was thinking as he traveled back to his father's house? He had told his dad off, taken all his dad's money and spent it in lavish, illicit living in a foreign land. He knew he was going to be ridiculed when the townsfolk saw him coming back in his tattered clothes. Maybe he was rehearsing what he was going to say: "I know I'm not good enough to come back as your son, but maybe I can live as a slave in your household?" Religious people tend to be so ritualistic and think there has to be a long list of things to do before God will accept them back into His house. In truth, no person is better than any other person. We have all ventured into a distant land. That is the message of the Bible. But the primary difference between Christianity and every other world view is this: "While he was still a long way off, his father saw him and was filled with compassion for him, he ran to his son" (Luke 15:20b, *NIV*). Once again, the western mind doesn't see this as that big of a deal, but the simple truth is that Middle Eastern noblemen never ran. Never. Aristotle wrote, "Great men never run, great men are run to." It's still true today. CEO's and Kings and Popes do not run. They ring a bell and people run to them. Children run, people who are in need run, desperate people run, people who are afraid run (husbands run), but not a nobleman and surely not God. The story that Jesus tells offends self-righteous people and in fact borders on the ridiculous. Jesus said that if you go away and blow everything, committing every sin under the sun, you can still run home to the Father and be forgiven. As soon as you turn your heart toward God everything is forgotten. The Father is so overwhelmed with love for you that He humbles Himself, forgets His own dignity, and runs to greet you. The Father does not see an offender. He sees a young man who's hungry and dirty and tired and takes off like Kobe Bryant on a fast break and sprints down the road to hug his son.

Meanwhile, the son is probably thinking he's made such a huge, unforgivable mistake, that the Father's sprint is intended to "keep him out" of the father's house. But then, the father hugs and kisses him with the type of emotion that leaves no doubt of the father's mercy, forgiveness, and love. Then, when the son starts to deliver his carefully planned speech the father interrupts, "No, you listen to the speech I have been planning for you since the day you left: bring the ring and put it on his finger, and my cloak, and put it on his back. You're not going to be a slave. You are my son! Everything that I have belongs to you! Kill the fattened calf, we are going to have the biggest party you have ever seen!"

It had never been about money, it had always been about relationship. I wonder when that thought finally dawned on the son. It broke the father's heart that the son actually thought that by living away from the father his life would be better. Nowhere in this text does Jesus say that the father said, "Now if you're willing to pay everything back then I'll let you come home." No, the father accepted the son back immediately, unconditionally, and with great joy and celebration.

IT'S TIME TO COME HOME!

I have two favorite authors whose books I read and reread. Ravi Zacharias, a personal friend, and Phillip Yancey, whom I have never met, are both gifted authors. Yancey, in his book *What's So Amazing About Grace*, records the following story:

> There was a girl who grew up with her father on their cherry orchard in Traverse City, Michigan. When she became a teenager, she didn't get along with her father very well. He was quite

conservative and didn't like the nose rings and navel piercings and short skirts that became a part of her everyday look. He grounded her a few times and the young girl got to the point that she was sick of her father's restrictions. She came up with a plan; she was going to run away from home. She decided she wasn't going to go to California or Florida, because those were the first places her dad would look. She decided to run away to Detroit.

Two days after she ran away she met a guy who drove the biggest car she'd ever seen. Everybody called him the Boss Man. He put her up in a penthouse suite, bought her lunch and let her order whatever she wanted from room service. She started thinking to herself, "Man I was right, dad knows nothing, and this is the life! His life is so boring!"

A couple of weeks went by, then a month, and the big Boss Man started teaching her things that men like. She was under age and Boss Man knew men would pay a premium for her. She didn't like it at first but she still had everything she wanted as a part of the high-party life. The Boss Man had given her so much, she didn't want to cross him, and so she did whatever he asked.

There was this one occasion where she became really frightened. She saw her face on a milk carton. She was terrified, but the longer she looked at it the more she realized that she didn't look anything like that picture anymore. She'd dyed her hair blonde and gotten additional tattoos and piercings. There was no way anyone would recognize her.

The Boss Man kept giving her little pills that made her feel better than she ever felt before. But after about a year she got sick. Then she started to get sick more often. This was a scary time, too, because she couldn't believe how quickly the Boss Man turned from loving her to hating her. Since she kept getting sick the Boss Man kicked her out onto the streets of Detroit in the dead of winter. She had no clothes, no food, and no money. She snagged a jacket and newspaper out of dumpster and started sleeping behind the shopping mall every night, close to the heating vents.

As the nights went by, she had to start sleeping with one

eye open, because there was a lot of violence in that part of the city. The nights were so cold that she couldn't find enough newspapers to keep warm. She didn't feel like a woman of the world anymore—she felt like a little girl again. She started crying, thinking about the cherry orchard in the spring, with the warm sunlight drifting through the cherry blossoms and the loving support of mom and dad.

She found just enough change to call home. The first time she got the answering machine; second time, answering machine; third time, still the answering machine, but this time she spoke. "Mom, dad, I'd like to come home now. Can I come home? I don't know if you think I'm alive or dead, but I'm going to come home. I'm going to buy a bus ticket from Detroit to Traverse City. My bus will arrive at midnight. If you're there, I know that you love me and that you will take me back. If not, I'll just stay on the bus and go up to Canada, and try to start a new life there."

The time finally arrived for her to get on the bus. She had seven hours to practice her speech and to think about what to say. The bus pulled into the station in Traverse City, the bus driver in an aggravated tone said, "You got fifteen minutes and then we gotta move on."

She got off the bus and to her disappointment she didn't see anyone. But then she walked into the terminal, not knowing what to expect. Not one of the thousand scenes that had played out in her mind prepared her for what she was about to see. There, within the concrete walls, seated on the plastic chairs of the bus terminal in Traverse City, Michigan stood a group of forty brothers and sisters and great aunts and uncles and cousins and a grandmother, and they all were wearing goofy party hats and blowing noise makers. Draped across the entire wall of the terminal was a computer-generated banner that read, "Welcome Home."

From out of the crowd of well-wishers strode her dad. She stared at him, tears quivering in her eyes like hot mercury. She began to deliver a memorized speech, "Dad, I'm sorry…."

But he interrupted her, "Hush child, we've got no time for

that, no time for apologies, you're going to be late. There's a party. There's a banquet waiting for you at home." [pages 49-51]

If you've been away from the Father, it's time to come home now. It's time to stop lying to yourself, pretending that you're home with the Father when you know you're not. It's time to get on the bus because if you'll come home, there's a big celebration party in heaven. Don't worry about what people think, just come home and the Father will welcome you with open arms.

Before we move on I have to ask you. How far should God be willing to go to bring you back into His house? Think again. How would you describe a father who knows the secret to ultimate happiness and success but withholds it from his children? What if your father possessed an infallible way to be a billionaire and allowed you to continue to live in poverty? What kind of a father would that be? Now, multiply that by infinity and you have God. He is so determined to give you the abundant life that He will frustrate your other pursuits until that they become secondary to the ultimate pursuit of living in the Father's house. So, we lose jobs, lose relationships and lose prospects. We don't get the girl, the guy, the promotion, into the right university, and, what do we do? We see this as God's abandonment when the reality could be that God intends to strip us of anything that is more important to us than God Himself. Whatever takes the place of God will never satisfy what it promises to satisfy, no matter how wonderful you think it is. This does not mean that any and all pursuits are somehow morally wrong. It just means that when any pursuit supersedes our pursuit of God, God reserves the right to frustrate or remove it altogether that we may come to the end of ourselves and return to the Father's house. So where are you living? At home with the Father, or, lost in a distant land?

GIDEON CALLED, GOD ANSWERED

Perhaps the most intriguing story concerning the manner in which God operates in us to draw us near to His glory is found in Judges 6-7. It is the story of Gideon. The Midianiates have been impoverishing the land of Israel for over seven years. Attempting to annihilate the Israelites, the well-trained warriors from the Midianite people were raiding the Israelite camps at harvest time, destroying the crops and slaughtering the livestock. This was genocide by starvation.

Finally, the children of Israel called out to God and He answered (Judges 6:7). God's first step was to choose Gideon to lead His army. Gideon is a reluctant leader because he is well aware that the odds are heavily stacked against him. In fact, the odds are better than 4 to 1. In Gideon's corner stand 32,000 ill-equipped, untrained farmers. In the Midianite corner stand 135,000 well-trained warriors looking for a fight.

Gideon must have been shocked to hear God proclaim, "You have too many men. I cannot deliver Midian into their hands, or Israel would boast against Me, 'my own strength has saved me'" (Judges 7:2). In other words, Israel may inaccurately assume that their own strength and courage brought them the victory. So instead, through two simple tests, God sifts the army down to 300 men. When 300 ill-trained farmers defeat 135,000 well trained Midianites, there is only one possible explanation—God.

This is the story of my own life and the lives of hundreds of people with whom I have shared stories. When the odds are so heavily stacked against me and I know the only way out of my predicament is God, something interesting happens. My prayer life intensifies. My willingness to go to God seems greater. My desire to be in the presence of God goes to another level. Alternatively, if I call on God and He powers up and immediately delivers me from my circumstances, my gratitude may be intense for the moment, but, my passion for Him soon fades. Day by day dependence on God results in priceless treasures. This is why I believe God is just as much interested in the process as He is in the final product. Intimacy with God comes as a result of time spent with Him. Time spent with Him allows God to reveal Himself to a greater degree. The more we know about God the less likely we are to seek our hope and strength in lesser loves or lesser things.

Judges 7:19-25 records the final moments of the battle between the Israelites and the Midianites, which are just as intense and unpredictable as a modern day thriller. When those three hundred men called on God in the midst of their battle with the Midianites, God answered. He sent confusion into the enemy camp and the well-equipped warriors began turning their swords on each other. Next thing you know, the Midiante soldiers were gripped with such fear that they began running away from the 300 farmers. This must have been a rather humorous scene. Thousands of spear-carrying, sword-bearing, armor-hoisting Midianites running scared from 300 non-equipped farmers who are shouting the name of the Lord! In the midst of this frightening battle, Israel was reminded of an omnipotent, omniscient God who often must strip us of everything we depend upon other than Himself before we can truly know God as He seeks to be known.

FRIEDA'S STORY

Recently, I met an angel. Her name is Frieda. Having recently been diagnosed with breast cancer, she is fighting the battle of her life. Frieda sat across the table from my wife and me, wearing a beautiful white hat to cover up the effects of the chemo. Her smile was radiant and her personality pleasant and contagious. My wife had told me that I should take the time to meet Frieda because "she's the most amazing woman I have ever seen." As soon as I sat down I saw a faced filled with joy and delight.

She spoke and I listened (a rarity for preachers) for over half an hour. She kept saying how Jesus had revealed Himself to her in a very special way over the last few months. No one is glad to be diagnosed with this horrible disease, but there was a part of Frieda that seemed glad to be in the middle of this battle. No, she was not in denial. She was well aware of the uncertainty and possible terminality of her disease. Speaking openly concerning the painful chemotherapy treatments, Frieda described how her husband had held her in his arms through an unbearable night of suffering.

Changing the subject back to Jesus however, she spoke of how God had given her a vision and a dream whereby she, like the lady in Luke 8 with the issue of bleeding, kept reaching out for Jesus to touch the hem of His garment that she might be healed. "And in my dream," she said, "I can see Jesus reaching out to me. Jesus has shown me that He is here and has never left me and He will give me the strength I need to make it through the pain. And when I need Him, all I have to do it call and He will answer."

Listening to Frieda reminded me of Peter Kreeft, and his comments concerning pain and the skeptic.

> "It is significant to note that most of the objections to the existence of God from the problem of suffering come from outside observers who are quite comfortable, whereas those who actually do the suffering are made into stronger believers by their suffering." [Lee Strobel quoting Peter Kreeft in *The Case for Faith.*(Grand Rapids, MI: Zondervan, 2000) 67.]

True isn't it? Those who suffer the most seem to know God the best. When we call God answers, but He answers in a way that catalyzes relationship, intimacy, and trust and faith in Him and His ability to give us what we need to fight the battles of our lives. As He releases His divine energy into our lives, we come to know the God of the universe in a way we never could have had we not gone through the valley.

REMEMBERING WHO GOD IS

Remember the movie *The Bear*? [Renn Productions,1988]. Separated from his mother, a little baby bear is adopted by a rather large and intimidating Kodiak. Throughout the entire movie, the cute little cuddly bear eludes the aggressive chase of a fierce mountain lion. At a rather climactic point in the movie, the chase appears to have come to an end and the little bear's demise seems certain.

Suddenly, the face of the mountain lion dramatically shifts from intimidation to terror. Carefully and slowly the lion begins a methodic retreat creating space between himself and the bear cub. You think, wow, *how could a full grown mountain lion be frightened by a little bear cub?* But then the camera pans back to a wider angle where you see father Kodiak standing upright, doing what he does best; scaring the beejeebies out of the would-be predator! Now, as powerful and effective as the Kodiak may seem, his power and authority pales in comparison to the God who chooses to take us through the fire in order to reveal Himself to us. Yet, even in the midst of the fire, His omnipotent power is there to sustain us.

CHAPTER 4

Upper and Lower Stories

Now, before we proceed with this idea of a loving Father who would actually do whatever it takes to get us back to the Father's house, even if it means bringing to frustration any hopes and dreams that are meant to replace what only He can give, we need to remember that there are always two sides to every narrative written into our lives: the upper story, and, the lower story. Yet, nothing has catalyzed the questioning of God's existence more than the series of unfortunate events that occur in the lower (earthly) realm. As painstaking as if may seem to some, we can not investigate the issue of Divine Romance merely from a subjective point of view. There must be definitive objective truth associated with any supposition and its ability to maintain its integrity. Part of that journey must include the admission that we are not God and do not necessarily know how our life ought to be going. Some things that fail to make sense to us make perfect sense to God in the larger scheme of things.

Again, Philip Yancey sheds a bright light on this issue in his book, *Rumors of Another World*. Yancey speaks of a mountain climbing experience in which he participates with some regularity. He speaks of how climbing mountains presents a "constantly shifting point of view!" At first there are walls of granite thousands of feet high which grant no real perspective of the surrounding terrain. Then, as one gets closer to the mouth of the mountain a thin path following seams in the rock become like lights that light the way. Appearing to be insurmountable at first, the journey up the mountain becomes quite comfortable as the path winds its way around the circumference. As the path zigs and zags, the view below constantly changes. Yancey describes how he sees Aspen trees on one side of the mountain, then discovering how these Aspens actually surround an Alpine lake as the view becomes more clear. As the ascent continues up the mountain Yancey notices that the lake and the forest nestle in a lush valley dotted with lakes, meadows and other groves of trees. He continues, "Later, I see that the valley fits into a cut on the side of the mountain and that the streams of water spilling from its lakes tumble down several thousand feet to feed a river that runs through a canyon near my home twenty miles away." Yancey's final conclusion is profound. "Only when I reach the summit does the entire landscape fit together. Until then, any conclusions I might draw would prove mistaken."

My frequent trips to Africa invariably teach me new things about the people and culture. One thing is a given: I never know with any kind of certainty which of my jokes will draw laughter and which ones will leave my audience with a blank stare and my translator with an awkward silence. Yet, there are a few quips guaranteed to generate the desired outcome no matter how many times I present them. One such short story tells of a man who is sitting under an acorn tree looking out over a watermelon patch. Mockingly, he speaks to God, "Lord, your sense of proportion seems to be all out of whack. Small plants, huge watermelons! Big tree, small little acorns! What gives?" Suddenly, a small acorn fell out of the tree and struck the man on the head. Thoughtfully, he replied, "Thank God that wasn't a watermelon!"

For some reason, this story always provokes enormous laughter and applause. I believe it is because the Africans do not struggle in the same way we westerners do with a God who would make decisions about our lives with which we simply do not agree nor understand. In the African mind God is like the Chief in the village. God is God and will do what is best for His people. And although we may not exhaustively comprehend what God is up to, we can always know with absolute certainty that He is working everything together for His good in us.

No mater how tragic or insurmountable things may appear from the lower level, God sees things we simply can not and do not see. He stands outside of time and space. All moments are present to Him. He knows the future because He is already there, and, He is committed to working everything together to accomplish His purpose in us. While conforming us to the image of His Son is indeed a high priority, we seldom remember that God's highest priority is Divine Romance. If conforming us to the image of Jesus was the highest priority, God could simply say the word and it would be done. But that's not what God is after. Without violating our freedom, He draws us into His presence and reveals Himself to us through some of the most difficult and tragic events of our lives. Then, when our eyes are opened and we begin to see God, true relationship and intimacy occur and God's upper story comes to fruition.

A perfect example of an upper story/lower story narrative can be found in the life of Joseph.

If you are familiar with the story in Genesis 39 and following, you are aware that a famine is approaching the land that has the potential to destroy God's people. God, rather than simply reaching down and touching earth and preventing the famine, decides to use the famine as a means by which to reveal Himself to Joseph in a way Joseph had not previously known.

Joseph's story is a sad one. The kid just can't catch a break! His brothers are jealous of the attention Joseph receives from their father Jacob. Their hatred for him is so intense that they throw him into a pit before deciding to make a profit by selling him to some passing Ishmaelites who in turn sold him into slavery in Egypt. In an attempt to deceive their father, the brothers dip Joseph's coat in animal blood and claim that a wild beast delivered a fatal blow to his beloved son. Meanwhile, Joseph ends up as a servant in a respected and wealthy business man's house. Mr. Potiphar is so impressed with Joseph's administrative skills and humility of heart that he places him in charge of the entire Potiphar Foundation. Although not an ideal situation, the Genesis narrative presents a Joseph who is patient and unswerving in his commitment to God. Unfortunately, Mrs. Potiphar, noticing that Joseph is quite handsome and well built, is unwavering in her pursuit toward intimacy of another kind. When accosted by Mrs. Potiphar and enticed to sleep with his bosses' wife, Joseph's reasoning concerning why he will not do such a thing is impressive.

> "No one is greater in this house than I am. My master has withheld nothing from me except you, because you are his wife. How then could I do such a wicked thing and sin against God?" And though she spoke to Joseph day after day, he refused to go to bed with her or even be with her." Genesis 39:9-10

Joseph refused to sleep with Mrs. Potiphar not because it would be a sin against Mr. Potiphar, nor because it would be a violation against Mrs. Potiphar, but because it would be a sin against God. Joseph does the right thing for the right reasons and where does it get him? In prison. That's right. "Hell hath no fury like a woman scorned." Mrs. Potiphar makes up some story about how Joseph tried to rape her and suddenly, everything is stripped from Joseph and he winds up in the dungeons of Egypt. From what can be determined, Joseph spent some thirteen years in the pit of this hellish existence. Yet, even in the midst of such horror, Joseph shines. Eventually he is put in charge of the entire prison, second only to the warden.

Now, it would be a mistake to assume that Joseph did not periodically struggle with his predicament. After all, one could make the argument that the more often he tried to do the right thing, the more his life continued on a downward spiral.

Time out. Our unrealistic expectations are often the source of our rebellion against God. Somewhere along the line we began to assume that if we do the right thing, God is bound by some preconceived covenant to make sure everything works out the way we want or desire. This is ridiculous. Once again, we think we know better than God how our life should be going. We do not. We are seldom privy to the upper story. Our calling is to be faithful to God and His purposes in the world even when things look grim.

The reality is that everyone who first comes to Christ does so to get something. That's perfectly natural. Man's search for meaning, purpose and significance will drive him to try just about any philosophy or creed. Some come to Christ in hopes that He will give them special insight or power that will lead to success in all their pursuits and endeavors. Others come to get forgiveness for their sins in hopes of being made right with God, and, being right with God, they think He will grant them access to divine power that enables them to latch on to their earthly hopes and dreams. "I hope that God can help me get that job." "I hope that God can help me get that girl!" "I hope that God can help me get that guy, raise, interview, child, career, position, or whatever else I may be pursuing." In short, we latch on to Jesus in the beginning because we hope that He can help us get what we really want, a successful career, an healthy family, a spouse, children, or anything else we associate with our happiness.

However, as time goes on, we are supposed to "be transformed" in our thinking. Instead of using Jesus to help us secure our real loves, Jesus must become the Love of our lives. We stop pursuing Jesus to get stuff and start pursuing Jesus to get Jesus. I have been writing about this topic for some time now. The more I write the more I realize what truly disturbs me about others, and, about myself. I wish I were immune to this type of thing but I am not. My mood or countenance directly correlates to the way my life is going at the moment. Problem is that I gauge the "way my life is going" by the attainment of certain pursuits that make me feel good about myself. What is the balance in my bank account? How are others viewing my significance? Am I making progress toward my life goals? Seldom do I define "the way my life is going" by "How close am I getting to God?" "Am I gaining on the character of Christ?" "Am I becoming more and more like Him every day?" Sad how these last three issues seldom impact my emotions or demeanor. I seem content with mediocrity.

This reminds me that I am still not wholly committed to pursuing Christ and His purposes in my life. The old man keeps creeping in, overriding my desire to give my all to Jesus with the intense urge to pursue the things that make me the recipient of praise and honor by the citizens of this world. Don't get me wrong! There is nothing wrong with being successful. But as a true follower of Jesus my greatest successes are not associated with my job, career, platform or bank account. My highest pursuit should be Jesus, period. All praise and honor should be directed toward Jesus, not me.

Yet, I find that seldom does the failure to draw near to God catalyze the same depression and anxiety associated with a low balance in my bank account. Ah! I see the real problem … I love Jesus, yes, but I still see Him as someone I am trying to get on board with my plan for my life. Therein lies the struggle of our lives. The conflicts we face are not always the attacks of the evil one but the tension God sets up in our lives to open our eyes to the reality that rather than spending so much time and energy trying to get God on board with our agenda, maybe we should be more concerned about getting on board with His.

As I read the stories of Moses, Abraham, and Jacob, the fathers of the Christian faith, I see three men who spent most of their lives trying to get God on board with their personal agendas. God tolerated their plans while at the same time frustrating their efforts. Abraham took matters into his own hands with Hagar. Moses did the same with an Egyptian soldier. Jacob made the same mistake when he stole the birthright from his brother Esau. All three men made the assumption that God needed to be "helped along" if His plans were going to come to fruition. This is always a mistake. Moses and Jacob found themselves running for their lives and Abraham's sin spurned a new nation that would persecute the people of God even until this day.

Bottom line? The moment we stop pursuing God for the purpose of retaining His power for our purposes is the very moment He can do His best work in us. This is what I see in Joseph. He gave up his life in order that he might find it. Even in the worst of circumstances, he held fast to his faith and faithfulness toward God.

Can I be so bold as to ask: what tension presently exists in your life? Is this a road block God established in order to get you to turn back from your own plan and submit to the way He has prepared for you? What decisions have you made apart from God that have brought disastrous consequences? Do you need to stop blaming God and take ownership of the choices you have made? Do you need to repent, ask forgiveness and ask God to get you back on the road that leads to life? What or "who" are you truly pursuing?

Back to our story. Joseph finds himself in the dungeons of Egypt suffering for doing the right thing. Yet, even in the worst possible circumstances of his life, God is still working the upper story to accomplish His purposes in both Israel, the people of God, and, more specifically, Joseph, the servant of God. Through a series of events, Joseph interpreted the dreams of two key servants previously employed by the king. Joseph begged these men to remember him upon their release from prison when they once again stood before the great Pharaoh. Both men forgot about Joseph so Joseph's downward spiral continued, that is, until one day when the Pharaoh began to dream and the cup bearer remembered Joseph the Dream Catcher! Through a series of events, at the right time and the right place, Joseph stood before the great king, interpreted his dream and became ruler over all the land of Egypt, second only to the Pharaoh himself.

In what must have been an astounding ceremony, Pharaoh announced to the people, "I hereby put you in charge of the whole land of Egypt." Then Pharaoh took his signet ring from his finger and put it on Joseph's finger. He dressed him in robes of fine linen and put a gold chain around his neck (Genesis 41:42). Joseph is now placed in a position where he possesses the power to feed the nation of Israel thereby sparing them from the likelihood and even possibility of extinction.

However, for our purposes here, in the context of Divine Romance, the definitive verse in the Joseph narrative is Genesis 50:19-21 where Joseph's brothers recognize Joseph as the most powerful man in Egypt, save the Pharaoh, and fear for their lives. But Joseph said to them,

> "'Don't be afraid. Am I in the place of God? [20]You intended to harm me, but God intended it for good to accomplish what is now being done, the saving of many lives. [21]So then, don't be afraid.

I will provide for you and your children.' And he reassured them
and spoke kindly to them."

Think of the years and years of pain and suffering Joseph's brothers had caused him. Think of all the times God could have rescued him. Think of every situation where Joseph did the right thing for the right reasons and suffered anyway. Yet, when everything comes to a head and the opportunity for revenge is directly in front of him, instead, Joseph chooses to forgive, asking the question, "Am I in the place of God?" and then revealing something that could have only been revealed to him through Divine Romance, "You intended to harm me, but God intended it for good to accomplish what is now being done, the saving of many lives" (Genesis 50:20).

Donald Trump was once asked, "What will you say to God when you stand before His throne?" Trump is reportedly to have said, "Hey God, you're in my seat." Most of our problems occur when we try to sit in God's chair. In reality, each of us has one of two choices when it comes to God: Obey God, or, be God. When we decide to be God, we live with a constant sense of disappointment and dissatisfaction because we think we know how every day of our life should be played out. The problem is, we have no real control over the details concerning what may or may not happen. Logically speaking, if it appears that we have no real control over our lives, then, the reality is that someone else does. Ultimate peace comes only when you get off God's throne, allow Him to be God and admit that you really have no idea how your life should be going in order for God to achieve His purposes and plan in you. This is the first reason Joseph was so successful. He truly trusted that God would work everything out for good in the end.

Therefore, if everything is not yet good, well, then, its not yet the end. Worshiping, praising, and trusting God in the midst of a life that spirals downward into the depths of prison is difficult. Yet, the journey along the way is the means whereby God reveals who He truly is. The only reason Joseph responded to his brothers in the manner that he did was because he had met God in the hell holes of Egypt and discovered that He was a gracious, loving, kind, and forgiving God who gives wisdom and grants stability during the most difficult times of our lives. He is large and in charge and will bring His plan to fruition. In the prisons, Joseph met God and was able to thrive, not merely survive, during a difficult situation, trusting that God is faithful to keep His promises to the people of Israel. And He used Joseph to save a nation, but, not without revealing Himself to Joseph along the way.

Joseph's story reminds me of a story my favorite author and friend Ravi

Zacharias tells about his close friend, Hein Pham, who humbly served Ravi as a translator during his time of service in Vietnam. After all the Americans pulled out of this disastrous affair, men like Hein Pham were rounded up, arrested, tortured and placed in prison camps. The guards at the camps had one mission in mind for people like Hein Pham: kick God out and usher Marx in. The brainwashing and torture of the prison camp proved to be too much for many. Hein was no exception. After much suffering, he began to question the existence of God. Finally, at the end of his rope, he vowed to wake up the next morning without kneeling in prayer to begin his day. That day, the guards assigned him to latrine duty. Forced to clean human excrement off walls and floors, Hein Pham noticed, during his daily rounds, that the commander was using pages of the Bible as toilet paper. As soon as Hein noticed the english in the waste paper basket, he picked it up, human excrement and all, wiped it clean and began to read. It was Romans 8:31-39.

> What, then, shall we say in response to these things? If God is for us, who can be against us? He who did not spare his own Son, but gave him up for us all—how will he not also, along with him, graciously give us all things? Who will bring any charge against those whom God has chosen? It is God who justifies. Who then is the one who condemns? No one. Christ Jesus who died—more than that, who was raised to life—is at the right hand of God and is also interceding for us. Who shall separate us from the love of Christ? Shall trouble or hardship or persecution or famine or nakedness or danger or sword? As it is written:
> "For your sake we face death all day long; we are considered as sheep to be slaughtered."
> No, in all these things we are more than conquerors through him who loved us. For I am convinced that neither death nor life, neither angels nor demons, neither the present nor the future, nor any powers, neither height nor depth, nor anything else in all creation, will be able to separate us from the love of God that is in Christ Jesus our Lord.

As soon as Hein Pham read this passage he said to himself, "There you go, God. You could not leave me alone even for twenty-four hours. Reinvigorated, he began building a fifty foot boat for his escape. One night, three men whom he feared might be from the Vietcong, asked Hein if he were building a boat trying to escape. Hein Pham denied the allegations and then went back to his room and prayed to God. "God, here I go again, trying to run my own life when you have clearly shown me that you are in charge. If these men come and ask me again, I am going to tell them the truth." Well, they did come again, within one hour of Hein's departure. They asked him, "Are you trying to escape?" Hein Pham replied, "Yes, I am trying to escape. Are you going to put me back into the prison?" The three men replied, "No, we want to come with you." Hein Pham and fifty others boarded a boat to escape by way of treacherous waters. Had it not been for the three men from Vietcong who were experienced, well-seasoned sailors, the ship would have capsized and all would have been lost!

We often make a grave error when we assume God's chair. We should never assume that we know better than God how all our circumstances should work out. Our job is to do what is right and to trust God for the outcomes. We are severely under-qualified for God's job. We simply do not have all the information. Besides, it is during the most treacherous waters of our lives that God reveals who He truly is and His ability to do more than we could ever hope for, ask for, or even imagine.

Joseph's life kept taking unfortunate turns but he remained faithful to his God trusting His providence and passionately pursuing a greater knowledge of who God really is. Nowhere in the Genesis narrative does Joseph question God's allegiance to him. He just keeps doing the right thing no matter what the result or where it led him. Even when God led him to horrible years in a dungeon, Joseph kept pursuing God. Even when he was falsely accused, sold into slavey and abandoned by his own family, still, Joseph trusted the character and nature of God he had been discovering from the days of his youth. Joseph let God be God and just kept walking. This is truly amazing given the fact that Joseph was only privy to the lower story. In the lower story, Joseph was going down, but in the upper story, the story that truly matters, Joseph's life was not spiraling down.

Years ago, someone gave me a copy of the best one hundred sermons ever preached on video. One of those messages featured an African-American preacher who wrote a summary of Joseph's life. I found it intriguing.

◆ Had Joseph not been given a coat of many colors, his brothers would not have been jealous.

✦ Had Joseph's brothers not been jealous, they would not have thrown him into the pit.

✦ Had they not thrown him into the pit, Joseph would not have been sold to the passing Ishmaelites.

✦ Had he not been sold to the passing Ismaelites, he would not have gotten down to Egypt.

✦ Had he not gotten down to Egypt, he would not have been sold upon the auction block.

✦ Had he not been sold on the auction block, Joseph would not have been purchased by Potiphar.

✦ Had he not been purchased by Potiphar, he would not have become overseer of Potiphar's household.

✦ Had Joseph not become overseer of Potiphar's household, he would not have been falsely accused by Mrs. Potiphar.

✦ Had he not been falsely accused by Mrs. Potiphar, Joseph would not have been thrown into prison.

✦ But had he not been thrown into prison, he would have never met the baker nor the butler.

✦ Had he not met the baker or the butler, Joseph could not have interpreted their dreams.

✦ But had he not interpreted their dreams, the butler may have never been released.

✦ Had the butler not been released, he would not have sat before the great king.

✦ Had he never sat before the great king, the butler could not have told the king about Joseph.

✦ Had the butler not told the king about Joseph, Joseph would have not stood before the great king.

+ Had Joseph not stood before the great king, he could not have interpreted the king's dream.

+ Had Joseph not interpreted the king's dream, he would not have found favor with the king.

+ Had he not found favor with the king, Joseph would not have been ruler over all the land of Egypt.

+ "Joseph wasn't going down. He was going up!"

Think for a moment how differently you would respond to the trials of your life if you could go to the end and see how everything turns out. Imagine knowing the score of the big game before you even watch it. Your favorite team is playing in the Super Bowl and you have the certainty of victory because somehow you were able to board a time machine, go into the future and witness the outcome of the game. Now, if you know with certainty that victory will come, when your favorite team fumbles the ball, throws an interception, or is penalized in any way, you simply take it in stride. After all, victory is certain, and, when victory is certain, temporary setbacks are exactly that! Temporary! At the end of the day, the real issue has to do with trusting the God who has walked between the pieces, the God who loves you so much that He did not spare His own son. This God can be trusted to have your best interests in mind, no matter how demoralizing things may appear in the present.

Let's get right down to the attitudes of our lives. Why are we chronic complainers? Because we think that we are omniscient. We think we have complete knowledge of the universe and how every thing should work at every moment in time to achieve a desired end. We actually think we know better than God how our lives should be going. I know that sounds harsh but only that kind of abrasiveness seems to wake us up. When impatience sneaks in and begins to dominate my life I have learned to ask a simple question: am I sitting in God's chair, again? This is man's great temptation. We want to be in charge. We want to be in control of our circumstances.

In fact, although its difficult to digest, the Bible tells us that we are at enmity with God. There is a hatred in us toward God because we want to sit in His chair. We want to be on the throne. Why are we so unwilling and still sitting in God's seat? Why are we so unwilling to forgive someone who has wronged us? When Joseph's brothers feared the most fierce revenge they instead became the recipients of a radical forgiveness. They begged Joseph, "Now please forgive the sins of the servants of the God of your father" (Gen. 50:17c). When that message was delivered to Joseph, he wept and said, "Don't be afraid. Am I in the place of God?" (Gen. 50:19a) In other words, every person who holds a grudge, holds onto anger or plans revenge is sitting in God's seat. "Vengeance is mine says the Lord" (Rom. 12:18), so get out of My chair. Only God has the right to exact retribution because in reality, we all deserve some measure of it. Therefore, if God withholds it from us, who are we to release it onto someone else. We think we know what "bad" people deserve but we don't. We have no idea what has happened to them in their lives or the kind of influences that have captured and bound them. We are unaware of what they have suffered or what they are suffering now. That does not mean that we excuse them for what they did or that we continue to position ourselves in such a fashion that would allow them to wound us again. It simply means that we get off God's chair, allow Him to be God, because He alone determines the outcomes.

Moreover, what men mean for evil, God determines for good. Ultimately, this is what sustained Joseph through difficult experiences. He explained to his brothers, "You intended to harm me, but God intended it for good to accomplish what is now being done, the saving of many lives." Joseph did not come to this conclusion on his own. He had met the One true God in the pit, in the palace, and in the prison. A Divine Romance had been taking place through every circumstance. Each time God drew Joseph in, he responded by running toward God, not away from Him.

This is the tragedy of so many lives. For many, when God begins to pursue through tragic circumstances, rather than embrace God and enjoy His goodness, they lash out at God like a jilted lover. They automatically assume that if God truly loved them, no harm would come to them. They want only mountain top experiences where everything is in full view. They loath life in the valley where the view is restricted, understanding is limited, and God feels like *theos absconditus*, the God who hides. The human view often pits the valley and the mountain against each other. God does not see life through this lens. In God's mind, the two are ultimately related. God is just as good and purposeful in the valley as He is on the mountain. In fact, the greatest strides toward our romance with God are celebrated on the mountain but seldom actually happen there. God needs the valley for that because only when everything is falling apart will we pursue the God of relationship knowing that what others may have meant for evil, God uses for good.

If we ever hope to know God in the way He seeks to be known we have to get to the point where we no longer choose to use God as a means to our ends. We must stop pursuing God to get things and begin pursuing God to get God. Second, we have to discard this western idea that life should be easy and that no trials of any kind should come our way. The Bible is realistic about evil, pain and suffering. The book of Job is completely subversive to the idea that if you are good, everything in life will be grand. Job was considered to be "righteous and blameless" and yet he lost everything. When he cried out for an explanation, God's answer was really quite simple and can be summarized, "Job, are you suggesting that in order for you to endure your pain, you are going to need full understanding of all these events? Job, there are thousands of things that happen everyday for which you do not have full understanding and comprehension. Your pain is no different. Get out of my seat."

Yet, by the end of the book of Job, Job says, "Before, I had heard of him with my ears but now I have seen him with my eyes." Wow! Job's own admission is that without the tragedies of his life, the death of his children, the total and comprehensive destruction of his property, the painful suffering of his physical body and the weariness and fatigue of his own soul, he would have never gone past hearing about God to experiencing God in a way that redeemed everything he had lost. "I know that my Redeemer lives and in the end He will stand upon the earth," proclaims Job (19:25).

This type of thinking is not at all foreign to Christ followers. In fact, the opposite is true. Take another look at the Joseph narrative.

> "Then Joseph said to his brothers, 'Come close to me.' When they had done so, he said, 'I am your brother Joseph, the one you sold into Egypt! 5And now, do not be distressed and do not be angry with yourselves for selling me here, because it was to save lives that God sent me ahead of you. 6For two years now there has been famine in the land, and for the next five years there will be no plowing and reaping. 7But God sent me ahead of you to preserve for you a remnant on earth and to save your lives by a great deliverance'" (Genesis 45:4-8).

Think of this now! Had all this not happened to Joseph, the Israelites would have become extinct in the famine! God uses the suffering of one man to keep His covenant promises to Abraham. This one man, Joseph, was rejected by his own people, sold for monetary gain, wore a robe dipped in blood, suffered for doing the right thing, saw his predicament as the will of God, and was estranged from the father he truly loved. Does this remind you of anyone? Jesus was rejected by his own people, sold by Judas for monetary gain, wore a robe that will be covered in blood, lived a good life and suffered for it, saw His suffering as the will of God to save His people, and was estranged from the father He loved. In fact, God gave up His own son so that He would not lose us. He turned His face away from Jesus so that He would never have to turn His face away from us. Through one man's suffering, God saved a nation.

During my time in New Zealand, I encountered many who had gotten caught up in a sort of health, wealth and prosperity movement. One young lady who had become quite irritable with me finally bellowed out, "My God is not your God, Pastor Jeff. My God would never allow His people to suffer!" Taken back, I asked her a simple question, "When was Jesus most centered in the will of His father?" She paused, looked at me and asked, "What do you mean?" I repeated my question, "At what point in Jesus' life was He most in the center of the Father's will?" Hesitantly, she responded, "When He died on the cross for our sins." She was correct, and speechless. The purpose for which Jesus came to earth was to suffer and die for the sins of mankind. Jesus' baptism was a crucial event in His life because this was the sign of His acceptance of His Messianic role. In His baptism, Jesus is publicly declaring that He will submit to the Father's will by dying to self-preservation and living for a purpose greater than himself. This is why the heaven's opened up and the Father spoke the words, "This is my beloved Son in whom I am well-pleased." Suffering and God's will are not mutually exclusive ideas. Just as He saved a nation through the tragic circumstances of one man, so also will He do some of His best work in you when your circumstances are unwanted, unfortunate, and unappreciated.

> "Our face shows grief but not despair,
> Our head, though bowed, has faith to spare,
> And even now we could suppose,
> Our thorns will somehow yield a rose.
> Our life with Him is full of signs,
> That God writes straight with crooked lines.
> Dark clouds can hide the rising sun,
> And all seem lost when all is won!"
>
> (Jeremiah Denton, *When Hell Was in Session*)

ONE FINAL COMMENT

I am a huge basketball fan. My wife calls me "the has been that never was." Although I am not a big fan of NBA basketball (I would much rather watch March Madness) there are a few players that come along from time to time that draw my attention. Passion and humility impress me no matter what the sport. Kevin Durant exudes both. Perhaps one of the most talented, all around, pressure immune players of all time, Kevin received the M.V.P. award a few years ago. His acceptance speech went viral largely in part for the words he spoke to his mother. After thanking the appropriate people, and God, he turned his attention to his mom. Weeping, he told his mother that he did not think she realized the magnitude of her influence on her children. He tearfully explained, "You had my brother when you were 18 years old." Three years later I came out. The odds were stacked against us." He went on to describe how his mother was a single parent with two boys with constant financial stress. They were ostracized by almost everyone they knew and very few of their acquaintances expected them to survive. Kevin and his family moved from apartment to apartment with no one looking after them. "One of the best memories I have is when we moved into our first apartment. We all sat in the living room with no furniture and hugged each other. We thought we'd made it!," says Kevin.

As the acceptance speech continued Kevin shifted his thoughts from the unfortunate hardships they were forced to endure to the recognition of all the good that came as a result. He spoke of how his mother woke him up in the middle of the night in the summer times, making me run up a hill, forcing him to do countless push-ups, screaming at him from the sidelines during his competitions. "We weren't supposed to be here, mom," said Kevin. "You made us believe. You kept us off the street, put clothes on our back, food on the table. When you did not eat, you made sure we ate. You went to sleep hungry. You sacrificed for us." Then, with a dramatic pause and tearful eyes, Kevin looked at his mother and said, "Mom, you are the real M.V.P.!" There was a standing ovation! Interesting, eh? Even we as humans know the value of hardships and how they shape and mold us into the people we become. God is no different. He is the Potter and we are the clay. Sometimes, when we mess up our lives so badly, the Potter has to take the clay, smash it on the ground, and start again. And he will, because He is committed to giving us the very best thing, Himself.

There are always two stories occurring at the same time in our lives. The upper story, God's Story in us and in the world, and, the lower story, the restricted view we have from the vantage point of our humanity and finiteness. Once you truly believe this to be true, you will submit to the work of God no matter what is going on in your life, trusting that He is large and in charge and is revealing Himself to you in ways you had not previously known.

CHAPTER 5

Trouble in a Distant Land

On July 25, 2015 I celebrated my twenty-ninth wedding anniversary. I spent the day writing in what used to be called Burma, now Myanmar. Robin and I usually spend the day together reminiscing about days gone by and dreaming about those yet to come. We talk about our goals and dreams, about our kids and their goals and dreams, and, of course, about how much we love each other and how we are growing old together. This day was different. We still mentioned some of those things in passing but my dear wife wanted to spend the day shopping the markets just across the Thailand border.

We have been married long enough for her to know that I would rather have a root canal than to fight the local crowds, haggling with shop keepers over a few dollars to get something that I will probably never use. Just shoot me now and get it over with. Robin informed me that it would be okay if I sat at a local coffee shop and continued writing while she stepped into a little bit of heaven. As I sat drinking my latte my mind drifted to the first time I met my beautiful wife. I was mesmerized. I had never seen anything so beautiful. Her ivory white skin highlighted by her dark brown hair and deep green eyes, along with an almost perfect figure, drew the attention of every male on campus. Immediately, I began to ask everyone I could find who knew anything about Robin Delaney to share whatever revelation they had obtained.

As a missionary kid, she grew up in N'dola, Zambia on the Copperbelt of Central Africa. She had attended the International School in Lusaka before returning to the states to complete her senior year of high school in East Tennessee at Daniel Boone High School. She was somewhat of an introvert, yet, she loved being with her friends dancing, shopping, or just hanging out. The word on the street was that she had dated a few guys but was weary of guys who moved too fast, not wanting to become just another catch for some dude who came to college to find a wife. This was helpful information. I played it as cool as I could given the reality I was hooked. Moving too fast would have been a fatal error, so, I gave her plenty of space right from the beginning. She appreciated that so much that at times she became the aggressor, calling me and asking about our next walk or movie, passing little notes to me on the team bus before we left for our next basketball excursion. It took me close to fourteen months and three break-ups to convince her I was the one. In my mind, I did not truly have Robin's commitment until the day of the wedding. When July 25, 1986 arrived, it was as much a relief as it was exciting.

Now, here is what we have said. God wants much more than for us to be in good legal standing with Him. He wants intimacy and relationship and is committed to making this a reality even in those seasons of our lives when we are not. We asked the question earlier, "How far should God be willing to go to save us from ourselves and from being sucked into the vortex of a world that gives Him lip service without full devotion?" If we stop and think about it for a moment, if God truly loves us and wants to give us every good thing culminating in an eternal existence of fellowship, intimacy and bliss, then, God should be somewhat aggressive in His actions toward us. Remember however that He cannot violate our freedom. To do so would be to diminish the integrity of genuine and authentic love. You can force a woman to do a lot of things but you cannot force her to love you. Therefore, God often pursues us gently at first, exhibiting an incredible patience, waiting on us to leave the distant land and return home to the Father. But as we get older, His efforts become far more intense not wanting anyone to perish but have everlasting life. Therefore, you may look back on your life and notice a pattern of what you previously assumed was God's abandonment, when in reality, God was coming closer to you, drawing you in through the difficult revealing circumstances of your life. This is the Divine Romance. He will proceed somewhat cautiously at first, but, the more the world draws us away from God to temporary finite pursuits, the more God will turn up the heat to ensure we have every opportunity to see Him as He is, run to Him, and forever be changed.

For me, God began to intensify the chase in 1990 when Robin an I were working as missionaries in Harare, Zimbabwe. As communicated earlier, I received Christ and went to a Christian University largely in part to a revelation God had granted me when I was working at a men's department store. But now God had called me to Africa to work at Zimbabwe University with Campus Crusade for Christ as a basketball coach and campus pastor. The thought of using basketball as a way to reach people with the Good News was thrilling and in fact a dream come true. God, however, had other plans. From the time we arrived in Zimbabwe things did not go as "we" had planned.

First, the missionary family with whom we were assigned to work had their work permit revoked and had to leave the country in ten days. This was devastating to my wife because the couple asked to leave was her parents. They had served in Africa for over twenty-three years, and suddenly, without any warning, Mugabe's regime began revoking permits and next thing you know, Robin and I are alone in a foreign country unfamiliar with the people or culture. Our only redeeming factor was that no real language barrier existed. Although Shona and N'debele were the indigenous languages, most everyone spoke or at least understood English.

With the pastors of the most effective and productive church in Harare heading home, leaders from the Mission group asked if I would be willing to become the Lead Pastor of the Greencroft Christian Church in the Capital city. The request felt more like pleading. There was simply no one else available for the job. I found the thought of this responsibility absolutely overwhelming. "Why would God do this to me?" "I am not prepared for this!" "I am not even sure I want to preach every weekend in any church." "I want to use the game of basketball, the talent God gave me, to do His work in the world." Those were some of my thoughts.

The night before my first weekend sermon, the nerves of what lay before me caused an "upchuck" of unseen proportions. "What had I gotten myself into?" "What did God expect of me?" And then, everything changed. I walked up to the platform to deliver the message and suddenly it felt like I was a fish in water. I could not believe I felt so comfortable, as if this were the true calling on my life.

As in my first encounter with God, I did not hear an audible voice but the words were no less real. God was saying, "Jeff, I have been with you from the beginning. I have allowed you to go your own way and make your own plans for the major part of your life. You have gone to college, played basketball all over the country, and experienced a relatively easy life. But now, it's My turn. I own you and and I prepared you for such a time as this. I have not called you to play basketball but to lead this church in a foreign country. You are not able to do it, I know. This is a good thing. You will need to rely on Me and by relying on Me you will begin to discover things about Me you had not previously known. Up until this time, most of your life has been self-serving. In fact, your relationship with Me has been self-serving. You have not been pursuing Me to get Me; you have been pursuing Me to get the things you really want most—money, power, prestige, and significance."

These words hit me like a thunderbolt because I knew there was so much truth in them. When I played high school basketball I was known as the praying player because just before every game I would make my way to the back of the locker room to pray for God's strength to represent Him well. Yet, down deep inside I knew that my prayers, although pure to some degree, were attempts to manipulate God into helping me play well that I might be noticed by some college scout and obtain a scholarship to play on a bigger stage, in front of more people, to be worshipped and adored. Even my calling to Africa had more to do with living a life above mediocrity and doing something that mattered, something that had the potential to change the world. Yes, I loved God and His Good News as well, but, every pure thought or endeavor upon which I embarked seemed to be tainted somehow by self aggrandizement.

Here's the thing; God is so patient. He knows our tendencies and will capitalize on them as a means to reveal Himself. When most people first come to Jesus they have high hopes that somehow He will help them have a better life. So, they seek God for their own agendas. Again, this is not necessarily a bad thing, an immature one, yes, but this is where we all begin. So, whatever your idol is that you hope God will help you attain, that is the very thing He will use to get your attention and draw you closer in. He takes the desires of your heart, breaks them down, exposes them for what they are until they are no longer ultimate things. He changes not only what you "do" but what you "want to do." But it takes a lot of time and frustration. And once again, the tendency is to think God has abandoned you when in reality He is closer to you than He has ever been before. He so close that you can feel His omnipotence breathing down your neck!

During my first few years in Zimbabwe, I prayed harder than I ever had before. The fear of failure haunted me day and night. My father-in-law, Charles Delaney, had accomplished so much in such a short period of time and I didn't want to mess it up! I begged God to grant me wisdom and understanding of the Shona people that I might bridge any communication gap that may have existed and spurn them on toward expansion and growth.

The thing with God is that I don't think He is concerned as much for "what" we pray as He is "that" we pray. Once He gets us on our knees, the revelation can begin. When God brought me to the end of myself, I began to seek Him with all of my heart, soul, mind, and strength. Yes, my seeking was still tainted. Rather than seeking God to get God, I was still seeking God to get God to do something for me, something that was important to my success. However, just because my prayers begin with a selfish motivation does not mean that they will end in a similar fashion. Once God gets us praying, anything can happen.

The real journey toward the full revelation of God began for me in 1990 and catapulted to a whole new level in 1992. God was breaking me apart at the seams in order to put me back together again, with a greater knowledge of who He is and how He works in the world.

MR. MASHONGA'S STORY

The people in Harare were growing with faith and vitality. Robin and I were on a spiritual high for those first two years until, for some reason known only to God, we, as a church, began to stagnate. We just could not seem to move forward. In the midst of our frustration, a little boy named Patrick in our congregation came to me one day and said, "Pastor, I'll tell you why the church isn't growing anymore and why things are just d-e-a-d!"

My first response, which I did not say out loud was, "Who is this little jerk? Does he not understand that I am the Pastor? I know all things spiritual! Who does he think he is...the little brat! This is all I need, some little kid telling me why the church isn't growing."

He continued, "Because Mr. Mashonga has not yet become a believer and until he does, we are stuck!."

Now, Mr. Mashonga was a tribal chief. Even though our church was in the city and established among well-educated English-speaking Shona people, the bush mentality was such a strong part of the culture that whether rural or urban, the Chief was still in charge. "You can take the African out of the bush but you can't take the bush out of the African," was a popular saying among both the Shona and the Ndebele. Therefore, just because the Mashongas and the people from their surrounding village had moved into the city didn't mean Mr. Mashonga was any less respected, honored, or adored.

Mr. Mashonga had two children: a son, Verice, and a daughter, Shingi, and both came to the church every time the doors were open. Mr. Mashonga, however, did not see the relevancy of our ministry, nor, did he believe in the One true God. Deeply steeped in and committed to Animism, he placed his faith in his ancestors and their ability to reach down into the lives of his people to bring both blessing and curse.

Patrick, hoping I would wake up and acknowledge the power of the Chief, pleaded with me to understand a simple truth. Until Mr. Mashonga becomes a believer who confesses Jesus Christ as Savior, neither will any of the other members of his tribe. Patrick was so passionate and I was so convinced that God had not called me to Greencroft to share the Good News with a few hundred people but with the entire city of Harare, nay, even all Zimbabwe. Therefore, we heeded his words and took immediate action.

I had learned enough about God through previous experiences to know that all hope is found in Him. The Apostle Paul had obviously discovered the same thing early on in his ministry when he said, "I came to you in weakness with great fear and trembling. My message and my preaching were not with wise and persuasive words, but with a demonstration of the Spirit's power, so that your faith might not rest on human wisdom, but on God's power" (1 Cor 2:3-5).

I knew that I had no "wise and persuasive" words anyway. What I needed was a demonstration of the Spirit's power, and so, I began to beg for it! I called for a church-wide prayer meeting.

For thirty straight days we gathered together, calling on the name of Jesus, asking God to work in Mr. Mashonga's heart. We prayed that God would orchestrate and fashion together events that would open his eyes to the Good News of the Gospel. I vividly remember explaining to God how this would be a good move on His part. "Lord, this must be your will! Do what You have to do to bring Mr. Mashonga home from the distant land and we'll set the city on fire with the gospel of Jesus Christ. Hallelujah!" I was fired up, inspired, and ready to receive a demonstration of the Spirit's power.

The thirty days ended on a Saturday morning when very early in the morning Robin and I were startled by a familiar sound at the front door. Its called a "knock" but it should never happen before eight on a weekend morning. Patrick, Verice's best friend, and the young boy who had given me the low down on Mr. Mashonga, stood at my front door in tears, screaming "Jeff, you better come quickly, Verice is dead!" "What?" "Is this some kind of joke? Verice is only fourteen years old. What do you mean Verice is dead?"

As we drove to the hospital Patrick explained how Verice had been injured on the rugby field earlier that morning. Tackled hard by an opposing player, his head had struck a rock on the playing field sending him into a coma. He now lay in the hospital's Intensive Care Unit with his family in hysteria not sure of what to do or who to call. My immediate thought was, "God ... what on earth are you doing? We've been praying for thirty straight days. Doesn't that count for something? Come on man! We asked You to move and orchestrate events in Mr. Mashonga's life, not to kill his firstborn son? You better do something fast or You're gonna blow it!"

When I arrived at the hospital and walked by the emergency room, Mr. Mashonga as well as his extended family, were waiting impatiently and weeping loudly as is customary in the Shona culture. As I passed by the waiting room on my way to Verice's bedside, Mr. Mashonga stared me down with a look of expectation that clearly communicated, "Okay, big fella, you say your God is powerful, let's see just how powerful He really is. Get in there and do something! My son is dying!" Suddenly, God's plan became crystal clear to me. He was going to raise Verice back from the dead.

I spoke with his nurse who informed me that Verice's outlook wasn't very good. "Neither was Lazarus's," I thought to myself. Then I began my bargaining with God. I don't remember the exact words but I do know it went something like this. "God, this is your big chance. I know that your desire is that none should perish but that all should have everlasting life. I know you know that Mr. Mashonga is a major player in the Shona culture and that his conversion would begin a domino effect that could only be measured in years to come. Don't blow this, God. This is our big chance to show Mr. Mashonga who the real God is. Like Elijah called down fire I am calling down a healing. Demonstrate your power, O God. Open the eyes of the blind. Let your Holy Spirit come down and provide the healing while I am in this room so that all will know that You and I are on the same side."

I prayed this prayer over and over for what seemed like hours. Finally, around 8 p.m., Verice died. In the Shona culture it is the pastor's responsibility to inform the family of the son's passing. I took a deep breath, moving slowly toward the waiting room, attempting to gather my thoughts. In a soft voice I whispered, "I am sorry to inform you that your son Verice has died." The magnitude of what just happened began to sink in. I felt an enormous burden as the family began weeping and wailing. Somehow I felt that all of this was my fault. I was even more overwhelmed with God's seemingly apathetic approach to the whole situation. I was sad and mad all at the same time.

When I released the news, Mr. Mashonga stared intensely in my direction. This time, I was unable to read the message he seemed intent on delivering. I noticed the pain and sadness, but there was something else, something not quite right, something indescribable, something almost surreal. Completely dumbfounded by all that had happened, I drove back to the farmhouse in which we were living knowing that in a few short hours I would be standing before the people of the Greencroft Christian Church trying to explain the events of the previous day. In my mind, this was God's perfect opportunity to show His power and presence and bring an entire family, maybe an entire community to faith in Jesus. I felt that we had done everything in our power. We had prayed diligently for over thirty days and nights. We had called on the name of the Lord Jesus expecting that the effective prayers of a righteous people would release God's divine power (James 5:16b). Instead, God never showed up. How would Mr. Mashonga ever come to know God now? How could my God ever recover in Mr. Mashonga's eyes?

That night, I dropped to my knees in my study and began to go one-on-one with God. I began to question if God even cared about what just happened. I just could not harmonize the God I thought I knew with the God of the last twenty-four hours. In my mind, there was no possible excuse for God's behavior. Maybe He really doesn't care about all people. Maybe He is too busy to be involved in every person's life or situation. Maybe I had God all wrong. Maybe He just leaves us to ourselves to make our way in the world as best we can, hoping that each of us will do what's right with little expectation that God will intervene.

Imagine my surprise the next morning when Mr. Mashonga did something he had never done before. He came to church. He came late, but, nevertheless, he came to church. Entering through the side door in the middle of my sermon he kept walking toward the front until he arrived on the platform, next to me and the pulpit. That's right. With a lack of understanding concerning protocol, Mr. Mashonga interrupted my message with a deliberate march toward the front of the worship center. Then, leaning over to whisper in my ear he said, "Pastor Jeff, do you mind if I have a word with my people?" Notice the emphasis on "my" people. These were indeed his people and he knew that I knew it and would never deny him the opportunity to speak to them. Denying him this right would have been hugely disrespectful and ultimately irrecoverable. So, I moved back to the chairs arranged directly behind the pulpit, yielding the floor to the Chief.

You can imagine the thoughts going through my mind at this point.

Mr. Mashonga, as his deliberate walk had indicated, was angry with me and disappointed in my God. He is obviously here to inform "his people" that this whole Christian thing is a farce and is ultimately powerless. Still angry with God myself, I put my head into my hands, defeated and demoralized, determining the time it would take me to pack up my things and catch the first plane out of Zimbabwe, because my ministry, for all practical purposes, is over, caput, finished, terminated, end of story; that's all she wrote! Sitting there feeling pitifully sorry for myself and passionately disappointed with God, Mr. Mashonga began to speak.

He began in a low humble tone but I knew he was just warming up. He said, "Most of you are aware that I lost my most precious son Verice in an horrible accident last evening. His mother and I are indeed saddened by this tragic loss. Our hearts are heavy and quite frankly, we are not sure how we are going to move on. However, (I thought, "O boy, here it comes.") I wanted to come here today to tell you that our son Verice loved this place. From the day he started coming here, he was a better son, a better student, a better man, (I lifted my head from my hands in sheer astonishment wondering where this was going) so I was wondering, if maybe, whatever you gave to him, you might be willing to give that to me, too."

The place erupted with love and applause. The thing that Verice had been given was Jesus and Mr. Mashonga was about to discover Him for the first time. I could not believe what just happened. Did I just witness Mr. Mashonga giving his life to Jesus? Had the Chief in a distant land finally come home? Yes, that's exactly what happened. In fact, the story gets better. After months of discipleship Mr. Mashonga became a leader in the Greencroft church. Years later he will become the Chairman of the Board of Elders and will lead the church into some of its best years.

Better still, Mr. Mashonga's little girl Shingi will grow up to marry the next preacher of the Greencroft Christian Church, Denford Chizanga, who will make great strides in compassion and evangelism, not merely in the community of Greencroft but in the city of Harare, nay, the entire country of Zimbabwe through a ministry called ADMT (Africa Development Ministry Training) where Denford and Shingi are training up new pastors, planting new churches and saving the people of Zimbabwe one village at a time. Most of the missionaries who have left Zimbabwe will tell you that no missionary accomplished in his or her lifetime what Denford and Shingi are accomplishing now.

I still see Denford and Shingi from time to time during my return to Zimbabwe each year or sometimes here in the states when both Denford and I are on the same speaking docket at various conventions. Every time I see him I remember Mr. Mashonga. But I also remember how God revealed Himself to me through Mr. Mashonga's conversion. That short season of ministry was an incredibly difficult season to say the least. I still wonder how God accomplished what He accomplished in all that chaos. Many questions remain. Did God cause Verice's death? That question offends many. Yet, life is a gift not a right. If God grants life, then, does He have the right to take it and use it for His purposes? After all, no matter what we experience here on planet earth, God can more than make up for in the world to come. Moreover, if God can make life the first time, can He not make it the second time? And is it not true that the life He makes the second time is far more glorious that the previous? Simply put, God always recovers because whatever is lost in this life is replaced to an infinitely greater degree in the world to come.

Regardless of one's conclusions concerning this event, I know with certainty that God's ways and my ways are quite different. And every time our methods come into conflict with each other, I learn something special about God. My assumptions about Him are often just that, assumptions. I find that I often create God in my own image failing to recognize that He is very different than I ever expected.

That day when Mr. Mashonga walked up to the platform and gave His life to Jesus forever changed the way I looked at God. The whole experience formed and shaped me concerning my ability to trust God when everything around me was falling apart. This is life isn't it? We want to know God's love, but that is impossible until we are in situations where we feel abandoned and unloved. We want to know God's miraculous hand, but that's only possible if the rug has been pulled out from under us and the only thing that can rescue us is God Himself. We want to know the wisdom of God, but that only happens when we have placed ourselves in drastic situations by the bad decisions we have made, then and only then, will we search the wisdom of God and discover that His word is a lamp unto my feet and a light unto my path.

The point is, you will never truly know God by merely reading about Him. God wants you to be experienced. True, you must be experienced within the confines of His word. God will not grant you an experience that directly conflicts with what He has stated in His word. Jesus said, "A house divided will not stand." When I was a young preacher I remember Charles Stanley telling the story of a young lady who said God told her to leave her husband and children and go to the mission field. Stanley showed the ridiculousness of this type of thinking. God would never give you permission to violate one aspect of His word in order to keep another part of His word.

I pray that God would do whatever He has to do in your life to reveal to you that no matter how bad things look, the same God that spoke the universe into being, when it was formless and shapeless and chaotic, is the same God who is able to take the chaos of your life and bring beauty, pattern and design into it.

A few years ago I was fortunate enough to attend the U.S. Open in Torrey Pines. I've got a friend by the name of Brett Mullin who was the 1975 U.S. Junior Amateur Golf Champion—and he's been milking it ever since. Every year he gets six tickets to the U.S. Open, no matter where it is, and this particular year he invited me to attend with him. Let me emphasize, these are not just tickets that get you in; they get you into the tent where there is free food. And I love free food. Brett and I had a great time. We were standing beside the 18th green when Tiger Woods sank that snake-like seventeen-foot putt to send the match into an eighteen hole play-off. Because I was with Brett, I was able to take in all the pleasures of the entire match on Monday—food and all!

As remarkable as that experience was, the best part of the trip was getting to know Brett and the amazing way God had worked in his life. I just love Brett Mullin. He is one of my favorite people in the whole world. Brett was raised to be a U.S. Open Champion. Similar to Tiger Woods, Brett was taught the game, and every aspect of it, by his father. Brett adored his dad. When Brett won the 1975 Amateur, everything was going as planned. Unfortunately, Brett's life took a hard turn. Shortly after his U.S. Amateur victory, Brett's father was diagnosed with cancer. The prognosis was grim and his father died within that same year.

Brett told me the story of how his life spiraled down from there; it was one thing after the next. He got married, had a child with Down's Syndrome who was later diagnosed with Diabetes and then with Leukemia. Brett went from job to job. In spite of being a sharp businessman he seemed to get into one bad situation after another. He would go from having everything one day to absolutely nothing the next, through no fault of his own. He was perpetually in those situations where his business partners were not treating him fairly.

A few months after he turned fifty he was diagnosed with Parkinson's Disease, and I could already see the tremors and the shakes in his hands when I was with him that weekend. There was a part of me that wondered why God allowed this man to suffer through so much. Why didn't God remove at least some of these hardships from Brett's life? It reminded me of the scene in Fiddler on the Roof, when Tevye is in the barn and cries out to God, "Would it spoil some vast eternal plan if I were a wealthy man? It's bad enough that I have all these problems, do I have to be poor, too?" Every time I looked at Brett I would wonder, "How much hardship is too much hardship?" And yet, Brett is one of the happiest people I know. In fact, I am not sure I know anyone who knows God as intimately and relationally as Brett.

I have played quite a few rounds of golf with Brett. I am always amazed at his ball striking ability. It is easy to see remnants of days gone by. What happened? Why did he stop playing? Brett told me that after his father passed away he turned to alcohol to numb the pain. He said that alcohol is like a snake—easy to grab, difficult to let go. Addiction destroyed Brett's golf game and any real chance he had to make his mark on the golfing world. In fact, alcohol came very close to taking Brett's life until one day he found himself at the end of his rope, ready to take his own life.

Before doing so, he cried out to God asking God to show him the way forward and to rescue him from this disease. To this day, I am not sure what happened in that bedroom that night with Brett but I can tell you this: Brett experienced a Jesus revelation. Brett said that he saw Jesus for the first time and knew at that moment that every thing he needed and wanted could be found in Jesus. This is why I said earlier that you will never know Jesus is all you need until Jesus is all you have. The question is, "Are you willing to allow God to strip everything else away in order that you may know the sufficiency of Jesus Christ and to know God in the way He seeks to be known?"

CHAPTER 6

Getting Closer to Home: A Mother's Prayers

Ever had that feeling when the phone rings that it is bad news?

I was on vacation with my family in Kai Iwi Lakes, just north of the city of Auckland in New Zealand. The prefix '001' on the Nokia screen indicated that the call was coming from the United States.

"Hello?" I said tentatively.

"Jeff, it's Jody. You better come home now. You better come quickly."

Jody is my brother, the youngest of the four Vines boys. The comedian of the family, Jody finds it necessary to begin every conversation with a joke he had recently heard at the local supermarket. This time was different. Something far more serious was on his agenda.

"Jody, what are you talking about?" I snapped back. "I'm on vacation with my family. Besides, I'm in New Zealand so I can't get anywhere quickly. They don't call this 'down under' for nothing. What's the problem?"

Jody's voice softened as he said, "Jeff, mom's not doing well. You better come."

"What do you mean 'Mom's not doing well'?" I replied incredulously. My mother was sixty-one years old at that time, the picture of good health. She was one of those mothers out in the yard playing basketball and baseball with her kids. She was blessed with the figure of an eighteen-year-old all her life, with very little effort required to maintain it.

"Mom just experienced a cardiac myopathy," Jody replied. He went on to explain that it is a condition that cannot be predicted. The heart muscle slowly loses strength, so over time the heart gradually stops beating. Mom had passed out because of the lack of oxygen to her brain.

"I'll be there as soon as I can," I assured my brother and hung up the phone. I told my wife and kids what was going on and then secured a plane ticket from Auckland to Los Angeles, then to Atlanta, and finally up to the Tri-City airport near my mother's home in Tennessee.

It was on those long, seemingly never-ending plane rides that my wrestling with God began, again! My silent prayers were filled with emotion. "God, this is a bad move on Your part," (why God doesn't just zap me out of existence I will never fully understand). I continued with my honest criticism. "I don't think You have thought this out completely. My mom is a good woman. In a world so filled with evil, I'd think You'd want to keep a few good people like her around."

During the thirteen hour plane ride across the Pacific, my mind flooded with cherished thoughts of my mom through the years. When the four Vines boys left home she decided that she couldn't just sit around the house. She had to do something and she might as well make money doing it. She worked as the head cashier of a little grocery store in our hometown of Elizabethton, Tennessee. Most teenagers would begin their occupational careers at this popular grocery store and my mom befriended every single one of them, becoming like a mother to them. I recalled that on occasion my mom would lend some of those kids money—or even just give it to them, along with advice (the advice came free whether they wanted it or not!). My mom was bold and courageous. She would share her faith with anyone who would listen—and often even with those who did not.

"This is a big mistake on Your part, God!" I pressed on with my argument. An idea came to me. "God, would it help if I gave You some options of other people I think You should take instead of my mom?" How about Miss Stover, our next-door neighbor? She is the devil incarnate, or perhaps, at least one of the lesser demons. Mean-ness was her forte. She was born with the gift of cruelty. She made it her personal objective to torture every child on Roan Street. What's worse, her property, including the cornfield next to our house, looked like something out of a Stephen King novel My brothers and I would play whiffle ball in our front yard and of course we would occasionally hit a ball into her garden. I would be the one assigned to retrieve it and I can still hear her high-pitched voice screaming and yelling, "Get out of my cornfield you little rascal!" To make matters worse, she had already poisoned two of our dogs and we were convinced she was going to poison us! Every time I fetched a ball out of her field, I imagined her coming out of the tall stalks, wielding a large machete, trying to chop off my head. O the fury in her visage!

"Lord, take Miss Stover instead. The world would be a better, safer, and kinder place."

Or how about the guy across the street who beats his wife and kids every time he comes home in a drunken stupor. I can still remember my father staring out our living room window at 2 a.m., listening to the cries of a woman and her children as the drunken dad released his fury on defenseless, innocent victims. Dad just kept praying that the wife and children would run out of their house and into our yard for safety. He always had a baseball bat firmly grasped in his hands as he prayed this prayer hoping that one day the abused mother and her chidlren would run into our house for safety and the drunken father would follow. "Vengeance is mine sayeth the Lord," my mother would remind my father. "Yes, honey, but sometimes God calls on one of His own to serve as the instrument of such justice! That's me!" he would respond.

"Why don't you take that guy, Lord? "Take one man, save a family. Take one woman, destroy a family. Your call."

The mental sparring with God continued until I arrived at the hospital where my attention shifted away from God and toward my mother. Gathered around the hospital bed, my father was expressing emotions uncommon to his usually stoic demeanor. My brothers, usually loud and demonstrative, sat in awkward and uncomfortable silence. No one knew what to say.

I was the preacher in the family. When I arrived at the hospital I felt a little bit like Jesus on one of His healing assignments. In that moment, all the events surrounding Verice's death came back in a intensely haunting fashion and the thought that like Verice, my prayers would remain unanswered and my mother would pass away, unnerved me. In fact, seeing my own mother hooked up to so many machines gave the appearance that she had already gone from this world to the next.

Moving closer to her side I remembered the belief that when someone is experiencing a state of comatose, the belief is that they can still hear the voices of those they love. So, in a desperate attempt to stop this horrible thing that was happening to my mother, I quickly grabbed my mom's hand, knelt down, and began talking to her. It must have sounded strange, because here I was, a grown man, talking with my mom like I was a little boy again. "Mommy, please don't leave me. Mommy, please don't leave me. I can't do this without you, Mommy. I need you. Please don't leave me." Nothing else mattered to me in this moment. I remember the nurses beginning to shed tears as they listened to my child-like cries. I was desperate now. My pleading intensified. I squeezed tighter the hand I was holding and repeated, "Please don't leave me. I love you, Mommy. Please don't leave me. Please don't leave me." Suddenly, a tear rolled down mom's face. No one was ever able to explain why that happened. The doctors had no answer for me. My Aunt who is a specialist in cardiac conditions had no answer for me. I was left to try to understand what was happening and I knew down deep inside my mother, in her own way, she was saying, "Goodbye."

After a little more time, I quietly left her room and slipped back into the waiting room to be with my dad and brothers. A few hours later the nurse invited us back into mom's room. "The end is near," she whispered to us. I went back in and knelt down one more time. Squeezing my mom's hand, I was pleading with her, though barely able to choke out the words. "Please don't leave me. Please don't leave me. Mom, I love you. I need you. Please don't leave me." And then, she took one last breath and went to see Jesus.

When she died, two things happened. First I didn't know it was possible to hurt as much as I did and still be alive. Second, my battle with God intensified.

"God, I know You were able so don't tell me You didn't save her because of a lack of faith on my part. I have faith that You are able. You could have saved her, so that must mean that You're not willing to save her and that's a bad plan, God!

"I can't understand, why wouldn't You be willing to save my mom? She's a good woman. This is an evil world. She served You all her life. Doesn't she deserve a little bit of help from You?"

What made me even more upset was that God didn't answer me. I, too, served Him diligently. I felt that God owed me. He owed the family. We should not be experiencing this kind of pain. My frustration only festered.

A few days went by and then it was time to go to the gravesite to bury my mom. It was cold, cloudy and rainy that day, which I felt was just perfect because it was the same way we all felt inside. The workers at the cemetery erected a tent to protect us, so the four sons and their father slowly marched in underneath it, taking our assigned seats on the front row. The casket was carried in and placed squarely in front of us.

I decided to make one last ditch effort to appeal to the Lord.

"This is Your last chance, God. Just like You did for Lazarus. You told his sisters if they still believed, something extraordinary could happen. God, I believe. Raise her up. You can do it. You've done it before. Look at all these people standing around this hole in the ground. Most of them are unbelievers. You could do a mighty work here, and, just like in the town of Bethany where Lazarus lived, perhaps many hearts would turn toward You, believe on Your Name, and my mother's suffering would not be in vain. With visions concerning the manner in which Verice's life came to an end and an unwillingness to accept that these events may end in a similar fashion, my pleading intensified one last time. "Come on God! Move! Do something!

Even now I will believe!"

I have told this story and in fact written a similar account in previous works. I retell the story here with a more intense focus on how the tragedies of our lives are not God's abandonment but His direct involvement in our lives to reveal Himself to us that we may know Him as He seeks to be known and therefore, experience all the byproducts that originate out of such knowledge. In the same way that Verice's death revealed a side to God about which I had previously heard but had not yet truly experienced, my mother's death opened the inner chambers of my own heart and allowed God to step inside, creating a much greater intimacy with Him and a greater knowledge of who God really is.

God has never spoken to me audibly, but that doesn't mean I have never heard directly from Him. As I sat by my mother's grave, waiting for the pall bearers to lower the casket into the ground, God spoke. "Jeff, are you finished? Now listen. Do you believe in heaven? Really? Could there be any better place for your mother right now? Your mom's not in that casket, Jeff. She never was. Does your mother want to return to you now that she's with Me? You talk about how good your mother was. What if I also noticed the goodness in her and wanted her here with Me now? Are you omniscient, Jeff? I thought I taught you this lesson already. Do you think you know better than me how your life should be going—how anybody's life, or death, should be going? Trust me. You are about to advance in your relationship with me. I am about to show you something that you would have not otherwise seen outside of this context. I have your attention. Now listen to me."

I was still in pain, but at least now I had something to wrestle with. I wasn't sure how the Divine Romance between God and me would go to another level but

I began to look for answers, and, in doing so, I discovered things about God I had not previously considered.

First, after my mom died, I realized that although God had revealed to me that He is able to work everything out for good and will indeed write His story, a good story, a story of redemption and restoration on all of history, I was still unsure concerning my place in His world. Sure, I am called to be a minister but there are thousands of us all over the world with various callings. I wanted to know my calling. Yes, God is large and in charge but what about us. He saved us, yes, I understand. But are we just pawns in His hands controlled and manipulated all of our lives to accomplish what God intends on accomplishing anyway. Do we have any real use to God? We have freedom in salvation but do we have freedom in sanctification? God draws us through general revelation into saving relationship, yes, I got that. But is our relationship with God one sided when it comes to serving Him? He is our Lord and master, yes, but we are also His sons and daughters. How does all of this work?

The death of my mother sparked a passion in me I had not previously known. There were so many questions that had been hiding underneath the surface that suddenly raised their inquisitive heads. How could I be certain that heaven is real? How do I really know that my mom is with God? Is this simply wishful subjective thinking or is there some objective evidence that points to this truth? My mother taught me that truth is found in the Bible, the Holy Word of God. But how can I trust a book that was written thousands of years ago? How can I be certain that today's versions of the Bible reflect the words that were originally written? How can I be certain that Jesus actually rose from the dead? What about all the pain, suffering, and evil in our world? How can we harmonize the Christian claim that God is good, merciful, and kind with events like the Holocaust or the Arminian or Rwandan Genocide?

In the years after my mother's death I was so plagued with these questions that the pursuit of the answers dominated my time and energy. Little did I realize that these very questions and the pursuit of the answers would draw me into a closer more intimate relationship with God. It's almost as if God knew exactly how I am wired and completely understood the kind of language I would need to hear to feel His love and to know Him more intimately.

As stated in chapter one, my love language is "words of affirmation." With every new apologetic discovery, I felt God's arms around me and knew that He was speaking affirmation directly to me. I have recorded my findings in a book I wrote entitled, "Dinner With Skeptics," another event that changed my life. I will not go into all the details here but if you need answers to some of the most difficult questions Christians are asked, I encourage you to go to Collegepress.com or Amazon.com and order the book. Understanding that most people are not wired in such a way as to experience God on a deeper level just because some of the more penetrating questions of life are answered, I want to hone in on something I know will hit home for all of us. My mother's death revealed more to me about God than any previous experience, even that of Verice's death and Mr. Mashonga's subsequent conversion.

✦ ✦ ✦ ✦ ✦ ✦ ✦ ✦ ✦ ✦

A couple of years after my mom's death I made a trip back to East Tennessee to speak at a conference and to visit my brothers. While there, my father ushered me into the back bedroom and gave me something very special. Dad said, "Son, I've been wanting to give this to you for sometime now. Its your mother's Bible and her favorite Charles Stanley devotional. She treasured these things so much and I am sure she would have wanted you to have them."

To my surprise, when I opened the book, a few tattered pieces of paper fell to the ground. Picking them up, I found scribbled on the pages four things my mother wanted more than anything else in this world. Four things for which she had been earnestly praying for years and years. Next to each item were little notes describing the request and how God had been granting them, and, the one's anticipated but not yet realized. As you read the first three, keep in mind the idea of Divine Romance. How did God use each situation to draw the person toward Himself? Did some run away to a distant land while others ran toward the father's house. No matter what the circumstance, we all get to choose. Its just God's way of protecting the integrity of real and authentic love.

The First Prayer was that my dad would know the love of God.

My father grew up in an incredibly violent home. His father was a WW II vet that never recovered from the war. He would often go into fits of rage, throwing things and cursing everything in sight. Unfortunately for my father, he often bore the brunt of my grandfather's frustration. Largely due to the frequent beatings received from his father, my dad developed a nervous stammer that would only entice his father toward more regular abuse. As a result of beatings with a shovel, my father walked hunched over for most of his life. In fact, I can never remember my father being able to stand in a perfectly erect position. The remnants of this abuse followed him all the days of his life. Shortly after the death of my mother, dad and I were seated on the back porch near his favorite grill where many culinary delights had been created over the years. During some good eats and the course of conversation my father opened up the window of his life and allowed me to look in.

"When I was a child, I never got any gifts or toys from my father," he explained. "Once, I did get a Christmas gift from someone, but it wasn't my dad. It was a little toy truck, which I loved. One day I accidentally left the toy down at the sawmill so I ran back to get it. I came to the top of the hill just in time to see a tractor run over my little truck, demolishing it." My dad told me that story with tears in his eyes.

Can you imagine the disaster waiting to happen when my mother, whose 'love language' is "words of affirmation," married my dad? What real chance did my father have of adequately expressing love to his wife? How could he possibly know how to love someone when such love had not been demonstrated or expressed toward him? Thank God my father had a mother who knew God as well as anyone I have ever known. She taught my father that He had one of two choices. One, weep, sulk and get angry with God over the fact that his father was a war-scarred, agnostic who had chosen to live in a distant land destroying his own life and wreaking havoc on every life around him, or two, run to God, acknowledging that God is often best seen through the tragedies of our lives.

My father chose to live at home with His heavenly father rather than the distant land common to his earthly father. As a result, dad broke the cycle of abuse, pursued God with a passion and grew in his understanding of God and God revealed a love with which my father was unfamiliar. I am not saying that his marriage to my mother was smooth sailing. No marriage is. But my father encountered every difficult circumstances with the attitude that God is always best seen in the midst of turmoil, and so, he always looked for God in the storm.

Consequently, when his marriage to my mother began to unravel, dad marched my mom off to counseling and learned how to express his love in a manner that would effectively communicate his care and concern to his wife. This type of fortitude inspired both my mother and her sons. When you see a man bound in the chains of a generation break free through the power of the Holy Spirit, you cannot help but to be in awe.

Although my father had learned to love my mother, mom was concerned that my father had not yet learned to receive the unconditional love of a Father who would never leave or abandon him. Mom lived with the fear that she had always been first in line in his list of loves. She understood that this had to change, and, that until dad began to pursue God above all other pursuits, he could not know every good thing in Jesus.

The Second Prayer was that my brother Tony would forgive her.

My mom had her issues, just like any other mother. She was not perfect. She was not Jesus. My mother's greatest mistakes landed on my younger brother Tony. Unpopular at school and uncommonly thin for most of her young life, she became the object of cruelty and ridicule. "String Bean," "Beanpole" or" Skeleton Girl" were nicknames hurled her way. Interesting eh? Those names are complimentary in today's world. In fact, in today's world she would be a model, a picture of beauty for the eye to behold.

Worse yet, mom grew up with an alcoholic, gambling father who berated her for anything and everything under the sun. To no one's surprise, Mom was not exactly the poster girl for self-esteem. My father, Obie Dean Vines, was a God-send. He treated her like the queen that she really was. Shortly after they were married, my oldest brother Timothy Dean came along, and then me, Jeffery Alan, and within fourteen short months, a third, Tony Wayland Vines.

As we grew older it became clear to mom that Tony was quite different than the first two. Unfortunately, the difference brought back painful memories my mother had never truly dealt with. Tony was not all that physically attractive, nor was he very athletic. My mom saw in him what her life had been, and suddenly, although I remain convinced not purposefully, she began to treat Tony different than the others. Interesting isn't it? You often become what you hated so much in someone else. She never really realized that she transferred all her childhood pain toward Tony. Every time she saw him, she was reminded of the pain she was trying to forget. As a result, she nagged him constantly. "Tony, why don't you eat healthier?" she'd say at the dinner table. "Why can't you comb your hair and take a bath?" Or, "Why can't you do better in school like your brothers?"

To make matters worse, Tony had the type of personality that said,, "the more you complain about me, the more I will give you reasons to complain!" He was as hard-headed as they come. I am not sure how Tony managed to turn out as well as he did. His journey toward manhood was not without obstacle and peril. He experimented with various coping mechanisms until he found a renewed faith in Jesus. Most today would claim he is the most handsome of the Vines boys. As most young men, he grew out of his most disgusting and debilitating habits. But the best move he made was to stop living in a distant land coming home to the Father. When he ran toward God rather than away from Him, he began to see every phase of his life as Divine Romance. What he never found in mom, he found in God.

To my mother's credit, however, when she realized, at least to some degree, what she was doing to Tony, she began seeing a Christian counselor. Then one day she began pursuing Tony's forgiveness. Tony, still reeling from what he considered mental and psychological abuse, instead of forgiving her, decided he was going to make her pay for everything she had done to him. This situation resulted in two unfortunate ramifications: First, my mom's ill treatment of my brother obviously caused great damage. When you feel like you are unloved by your mother it leads to a life-long struggle. Lack of love breeds insecurity. Insecurity breeds anger. Anger breeds self hate. Self hate breeds porcupines. Have you ever tried to hug a porcupine? You cannot love someone who does not love himself. I've seen young women marry these men in an attempt to rescue them, but you can't love someone until that person learns to love himself. Here's the second result we observed. Because Tony was so bitter and unwilling to forgive my mom, everyday his wound would go deeper and deeper. That's the problem with seeing yourself as a victim— every time you see the person that's hurting you, the wound deepens and festers.

The night my mom died, Tony was at the hospital but not at her bedside. When I noticed his absence I became genuinely concerned that reality of her death coupled with the reality that what she wanted more than anything else in her later years was his forgiveness, might send him over the edge. Running through the poorly lit corridors of the hospital searching for my brother, I finally found him in a dark corner, curled up in the fetal position. "Tony, what are you doing?" I asked. "What's wrong?" Looking down at the cold floor tile, all he could do was mumble, "My mommy is dead. My mommy is dead. My mommy is dead."

I got down on the floor and held him in my arms. While I tried to comfort him, it occurred to me that the cost of unforgiveness is a price far too high to pay. Tony will live the rest of his life knowing that the one thing his mother wanted most from him, he was never willing to give, until it was too late.

The Third Prayer was that her sons would love one another.

How many mothers pray that prayer? We were so close as young children.

It was a great family—still dysfunctional—but we were very close. I have many wonderful family memories. We would go up to Mountain City, Tennessee, to see the rhododendrons when they were in bloom. We'd take in all that beauty while eating boloney sandwiches and drinking Pepsi out of those old glass bottles. We'd play baseball together in the front yard. Our place seemed to be the gathering place for all the neighborhood kids, especially in the summer when we played baseball. My mom was the pitcher and my dad was the catcher. It was so much fun we didn't even mind the summer heat. We fought, no mistaking that point. But we loved each other.

When we got older, we started to grow apart because we were immature and proud. My oldest brother got married and had children, which suddenly caused the other three brothers to think they were professionals on how to raise kids. Before long we all got married and had kids of our own, and of course remained experts at what was wrong with every one else's kids, save ours. When we would get the whole family together, the tension was thick. What are you going to say about my child? My son is better than yours! Add political disagreements between Republicans and Democrats and don't forget Sunday afternoon discussions on religion with a Baptist, a Pentecostal, a non-instrumental Church of Christer, and me, obviously the only sane one. We fought so much we broke our mother's heart.

After one family picnic my mom broke down in tears. Leaning her head on my shoulder I gently asked, "What's wrong, mom?" "I just want you kids to love each other," she replied through tears. That's when it hit me—that was why she did the Thanksgiving meals and the Christmas dinners. Not because she enjoyed working all day and then coming home and cooking for hours and hours. Not because she wanted to try out new recipes from the Betty Crocker Cookbook. She was trying to hold the family together. She was hoping that over time we'd come together and finally grow up. She wanted us to enjoy each other and forgive each other and live our lives caring for one another after she was gone.

The Fourth Prayer was that Jeff would love people as much as he loves teaching.

After that same family picnic, my mom took me aside and said, "Jeff, I want to talk to you. I've got some concerns. "I'm okay, mom. I'm fine," I answered. Thinking she was still bothered by the conversations the brothers were having around the table, I added, "You know how your children get defensive with each other. I'm alright."

She had something different on her mind. "No you're not alright. I know you, because you're just like me. I'm concerned that your love and passion for teaching and preaching is not equal to your love and compassion for people. Let me tell you something, you'll never make it in ministry until you learn to love people with the same passion you love the Word." Wow! That hurt. Problem is, I knew she was right and now she had said it.

Confronting me must have been extremely difficult for her. I know, as do all my brothers, that I was the favored son. Who knows why really. I could not see it when we were young, but, looking back, I can now easily see what my brothers have been saying for years. For some reason which no one knows, mom favored me. She loved all her sons but there is no doubt she took my side and leaned in my direction when conflict occurred. And now, here she was giving me a little corrective criticism. She was genuinely concerned and she had a right to be.

Any pastor worth his salt admits the struggle between building Christ's kingdom and building our own. If we are not careful we will manipulate people to achieve less than godly goals. As with the rest of the human race, we often find our significance in the size of our churches or the level of our financial contributions. This is precisely why there are times God strips pastors from their congregations in order to get them back to their first love. How many times in my life have I pursued God not for the sake of gaining God but for the sake of getting God to grow my church so that I could be praised and worshiped? This is a dangerous game. God is not going to share His glory with anybody, including well-meaning, well-intentioned pastors. My mother loved me enough to not only confront me but to also pray for me.

Now, here is what's so captivating concerning my mother's passion. As I sat down to read each of these prayer requests, it dawned on me that every single one of them had been answered and that they had come to fruition in and through her passing.

Let's begin with my father. My dad and I were sitting on the front porch of the family home a few days after my mom's passing. For the first time that I could remember, he spoke to me as Pastor Jeff rather than Jeff, his second born son. He complained, "Why, son? "Why did God take your mother from me?" I could see his wheels turning trying to make sense of it all. Yet, ten years later, just a few years before his own death, dad invited me to the back porch of our home and told me how God had revealed a love for him that he had never known after mom's death. I could see such a change in him. A father that struggled to say, "I love you," to his children now spoke words of love and affection with sincerity and ease. Had my father not lost his wife, he would have forever looked to her as his savior and never really known what it was like to be loved eternally and unconditionally.

I am not saying that God looked down one day and decided to remove my mother from planet earth. I am simply saying that God is large and in charge and knows every past, present, and future event and continues to use every event of our lives to divinely court and engage us toward a deeper and more intimate relationship with Him. Where my father is concerned, mom's number one prayer eventuated primarily due to her own passing from this life into the next.

Second, my mother's passionate prayer that some day her third son would be able to forgive her also became a reality when she passed away. Suddenly, Tony's eyes were opened to his mother's love for him. The most beautiful thing about my mother's funeral was the artistic mural timeline created and displayed by Tony Wayland Vines. It was fantastically and beautifully arrayed. When I saw it I wept. From the moment that Tony lost his mother he came out of the distant land choosing to live at home with the Father, and, the more He was exposed to the Father's grace and forgiveness in his own life, the more complete and full his forgiveness toward mom.

In fact, Tony now sees all of this as Divine Romance, God's way of drawing him into the love relationship he had so desperately been seeking with his mother. Had Tony received the significance and self-esteem for which he longed from His mother, he probably wouldn't have searched for it in God. Now, one must be careful here. That does not mean that father's and mother's are excused from abandoning their children. It simply means that what man means for evil, God can use for good. This is precisely why we never play the role of victim. Instead, admitting our lack of omniscience, we trust that God is working on every side of every circumstance to bring us into a closer, more intimate relationship with Him and a deeper revelation of who He actually is.

My father, through the death of His wife, discovered the God who loves and cares for His own. My brother Tony, through the death of his mother, discovered the God who shows incomparable mercy and grants us all the significance and self-esteem we could ever hope for.

And what about the relationship between we four Vines boys? There can be no doubt that the death of our mother left us searching for the clue that could hold our families together. When our mother died, each of us realized to a greater degree our own mortality. We began to see more clearly that there were no guarantees in this life, and, despite our differences, we were one in Christ. And He is the Christ who defeated death and enables us to see our mother again. Mom's death galvanized our relationship with each other and with our father and reminded us of God's call to live our lives for something greater than ourselves, not for our kingdom and our selfish purposes but for the kingdom that is to come and for the purposes of God in Christ.

Suddenly, we put our petty differences aside and as each of us pursued God for comfort we found that God's calling on our lives included comforting each other. Each of us discovered both the God of comfort and the God of relationship. Once again, through the horrible experience of losing our mother, we discovered things about God that we had previously known but of which we had never truly felt or experienced.

And then, there was me. What about me? What about my mom's concern for my superficiality and self-aggrandizement without genuine and authentic care, concern, and compassion for others? Well, there's a part of me that wishes my mother had never prayed that prayer. Evidently I am a slow learner and God is a patient teacher, not willing that I should forfeit that which He has called me to do. Since the death of my mother, God has been determined to reveal Himself to me in ways that would enhance my calling. There are so many examples to give. The next chapter will reveal the most difficult season of my life, a season in which I believed that the end of my life was very near. As you make your way through that chapter, remember two things: one, my mother's prayer and two, remember that it is possible to be in the absolute worse place in your life and still be in the very center of God's will. (See Jesus on the cross).

CHAPTER 7

My Personal Rainstorm

"You must embrace the rains!"

It was not only what Godfrey said but how he said it. The enthusiastic support of bad weather took me by surprise. It shouldn't have, however. There were many things viewed differently in Africa than they were back home in the United States.

Godfrey made his living as a gardener. I was living in Africa, doing work among the Shona tribe in the country of Zimbabwe when the two of us became friends.

I vividly recall the first time I heard him make that statement. I was complaining to him about the heavy rains we were experiencing in Harare. He looked at me wide-eyed with surprise and stated rather emphatically, "No boss! You must embrace the rains!"

"What?" I responded, not certain I had heard him correctly.

"Yes, you must embrace the rains!" he repeated. "The rains are necessary to wash away the chaff and clear the way for a great harvest!"

I soon realized that Godfrey, 100% Shona, did not merely apply this principle to planting, growing and harvesting crops, but, to every facet of life. "Heavy rain," he said, "must come to every life, washing away all that chaff that chokes out the life God designed for us to live." Imagine what lies behind this kind of thinking. God does not merely allow the rain! He sends the rain! He does not merely tolerate the storm. He often causes the winds and waves to crash down upon us for a greater good—in fact—for *our* greater good—to remove that which continues to choke out the life He intended us to live.

Deep within the African people is the belief that bad times, bad things, and other unfortunate events are necessary to strengthen and mature the family unit as a whole. Suffering is almost never seen as God's abandonment. In my years of ministry in Zimbabwe I never once heard someone question the existence of God in the midst of horrific suffering. My friends in Africa never felt it necessary to offer an exhaustive explanation concerning the "why" of unfortunate events. Instead, they assumed pain and struggle were simply a necessary part of the present creation scenario and essential to what the Creator of the universe was trying to accomplish on planet earth. They seemed to understand their finiteness and thus their limitation.

There can be no doubt whatsoever that the will of God is that you live a life of abundance. Jesus said He came that we may have life and have it to the full. However, the road to the abundant life is often shaped and formed by the heavy rains that deepen the path and make the way clear.

Our response to the rains make all the difference in the world. And our response to the rains has everything to do with whether or not we see the rains as "friend" or "foe."

+ We resist and fight against foes.

+ We embrace and learn from friends.

If the Shona are correct in their worldview, then the only people who need no rain are those who have no chaff in their lives. Rain, in other words, is from Heaven above and our response to it must consider this one simple truth Godfrey expressed to me that day: "heavy rain," he said, "must come to every life, washing away all that chaff that chokes out the life God designed for us to live." Again, we must assume that it is quite possible to be under the threat of heavy weather—even ferocious storms, while at the same time, being directly in the center of the will of God. If Christ is our Example, then, for Heaven's sake, let Him be! At what point in Jesus' life was He most in the center of His Father's will? The cross, right? Yet, this was also the most difficult time of Jesus' life. The Bible tells us that He was so anxious previous to the cup of pain and suffering He was about to drink that He began to sweat drops of blood. This is an actual medical condition called, hematidrosis in which the capillaries burst mingling blood with sweat. Such a condition can lead to death and at the very least makes the skin incredibly sensitive to touch twenty-four to forty-eight hours after the experience. Considering the fact that Jesus is about to be beaten and scourged shortly after His Garden of Gethsemane experience, the last few days of Jesus' life must have felt like the mother of all rain storms. Yet, in the midst of all of this, Jesus was right where God wanted Him to be.

Through Christ's obedience, God accomplished His greatest work—the salvation, redemption and reconciliation of mankind back to Himself. Consequently, the greatest feat ever accomplished on planet earth required the suffering of the One who least deserved it.

Our perspective on pain and suffering in the west has often short-circuited the work of God in our lives. It's prevented God from using us to accomplish great things. It's closed our eyes to the reality of who God is and how He works in our world. And, it's ultimately robbed us of the sense of beyond, for which we all so desperately long.

Believe it or not, if I could choose any place I could be right now, it would be Zimbabwe, Africa. Yes, I am aware of all the pain and suffering Mugabe's regime has inflicted on the Shona people, the indigenous people, of this fertile, abundant land in central Africa. Yet still, it remains one of the most beautiful places on the planet. Moreover, even though the Shona and Ndebele people have been through so much over the last twenty years, the smiles remain and the hospitality continues.

Once a year I make my way across the Atlantic and head toward the prisons of Rwanda for four days of leadership training and then finally on my way to what was once called, "The Bread Basket of Africa," anticipating another meandering hike through Victoria Falls and a short respite from the work load back in Los Angeles.

A few years ago, things were going as planned. I enjoyed ten days in Harare teaching, preaching and golfing. Seated at my favorite cafe with only a few days left before I would fly back to southern California to continue the grueling, yet fulfilling, work of ministry, I finished my cafe mocha and stood up to take a quick break from sermon prep when suddenly, with my heart racing, my vision unclear and my balance all out of whack, I literally fell to the floor. I thought, "Oh no, this is it. I am having a heart attack!"

I tried to take a few steps but could not. I sat down on the steps begging the world to stop spinning around and asking God to make this thing go away. But it would not. I felt dizzy, disoriented and debilitated. I just sat there wondering what to do. Thousands of miles from home with no idea of what was happening to me, I began to pray. "Please God, this can't be it. Not here! Not now! Please take this away! Please . . ."

Finally, I gained the presence of mind to get into my truck and drive back to the lodge where I was staying. The fifteen-minute drive was the most challenging of my life. It felt as though any minute I would keel over, pass out and then what? Thankfully, I made it back to the lodge to discover that the manager actually had nursing experience. I shared with her my symptoms and she rushed me into her makeshift office, quickly took my blood pressure and then escorted me to her Land Rover. On the way to the private medical clinic she told me that my blood pressure was 190 over 140. In other words, stroke level.

The Zimbabwean doctor quickly gave me a magical injection that within twelve minutes brought me back to some sense of normalcy. He then began to ask me a series of what seemed like foolish questions, all of which drew the same response from me, "no."

"Do you have a history of high blood pressure?"

"No."

"Do you have any heart condition?"

"No."

"Do you have any history of diabetes?"

"No."

"Do you have periods of fainting?"

"No."

"Do you sometimes find yourself forgetting important events?"

I thought, "Dude! Really?" Everybody forgets important events. Most of the time it is associated with selective hearing. I often forget when my wife says, "Take out the trash. Pay the bills. Feed the dog. Mow the lawn. Buy some milk and bread."

Finally, after a flood of questions I said, "Look at me doc. I run four miles three times a week. I work out at the gym three times a week. I watch carefully what I eat. My weight has not changed in thirty years. I am still six feet-four inches tall and 200 pounds. I run, bike, swim, hike, golf. I have no history of any medical problems whatsoever. So doc, what is wrong with me?"

He quickly replied, "I don't know but I am going to find out."

After running test after test he came into the waiting area, escorted me back to his office and said, "Pastor Jeff, there is nothing wrong with you."

You would think I would be relieved but I wasn't. I wanted an explanation for what happened to me. Moreover, I wanted assurance that it would never happen again. Instead, he sent me back to the lodge with three little pills I was supposed to take if the symptoms reappeared. Well, they did! This next time they were far more intense. The owners of the lodge rushed me back to the emergency room, where the doctors gave me another shot and just waited. Thank God, the sweet little concoction worked again!

By this time, I was an emotional wreck! Thousands of miles away from home unsure what in the world was happening to me. I phoned my father in law and he told me to immediately change my flight and get back to Los Angeles as soon as possible. I sent a text to my friend Ravi Zacharias and he repeated the same advice. His text read, "Jeff, this does not sound good. Get back to LA as soon as you can, Godspeed!"

Good advice, only one little problem. "As soon as possible" would take about twenty-four hours of plane rides, airport lounges, and long lines at airline gates. The thought of sitting in a confined space thirty thousand feet above the ground terrified me. What if I have another attack? What if my blood pressure soars and there is no doctor's magic shot to make everything okay? What if I suffer a paralyzing stroke or worse yet, even death?

My mind was spinning and my fears were growing which seemed to make everything that much worse. Finally gaining the courage to call the airline, make the changes, and step on board the aircraft, we took off from Harare on our way to Johannesburg, South Africa, then on to London and finally Los Angeles.

While in the Air France Lounge in Jo'burg, waiting on the flight to London, the hellish feeling returned. My blood pressure soared. My pulse seemed out of control. I could not stand. I felt completely overwhelmed. The best way I can describe this feeling is to imagine that you are tied to the railway tracks and an oncoming train is just a few hundred feet away and there is nothing you can do about it. Some call it the feeling of impending, imminent doom! Or, for those of you who are not so dramatic, it's like feeling the effects of a hundred yard sprint without ever actually moving out of your chair. The heart is racing. The blood is pumping, Yet, you're not moving. You are perfectly still.

I began to pray, "God, please. Not here. Don't let me die here. Not in this Air France airport lounge. At least move me over to a respectable, heroic lounge like British Air. Don't let me die in a lounge known for its pacifist, non-active, noncommittal attitude. Its just not me!"

Okay, I can joke now but trust me, it wasn't funny then. Hesitantly, I took one of the pills the doctor in Zimbabwe gave me and to tell you the truth I do not remember much after that until we landed in London. Still groggy from the after-effects of the medical magic, I made my way toward the British Air Lounge, had some breakfast and waited for the next attack to come. Thank God it did not.

I made it to Los Angeles thinking that perhaps once I got home everything would settle down. Perhaps I had contracted some virus in Africa that needed to run its course. Perhaps I just needed some time to heal. Unfortunately, things did not work out that way.

My first night back home was intense. My family rushed me to the Emergency Room. The trip from the parking lot to the ER was like learning to walk again. With every step came the overwhelming feeling that I could not take the next one. Once I arrived they rushed me back to the doctor's office. The wise and experienced Asian doctor came in and listened to my story then responded, "We need to do some tests right away." I thought, "Yes, finally we will get to the bottom of this and I will be ready to get back on my feet and live my life!"

Unfortunately, the next six months of my life were by far the worst. The attacks continued almost every night. My children had never seen their father like this and were concerned. I remember one particular evening taking the family to dinner and a movie, only, we never made it to the movie. During mealtime, the overwhelming, debilitating feeling returned. I could feel my blood pressure rising and my pulse racing. The world was closing in on me and I needed to get out of the restaurant. My teenage children saw what was happening to me and although they said they understood why it was necessary to return home I could not help but notice both their disappointment and concern. Over the next months this would become commonplace in my life and theirs.

In fact, the energy and passion required to lead a mega-church can often be taxing. Throw in some health issues and now we've really got a problem. There were times just before I went up to preach that fear and anxiety would take hold of me and my Executive Pastor would have to remind me that with Christ all things are possible.

On one particular occasion, Easter Weekend at the Felix Event Center at Azusa Pacific University, ten thousand people came expecting to hear a message from their Senior Pastor. As I sat waiting in the Green Room, that familiar feeling began to creep in. This time, I remained silent and simply tried to deal with it internally. But the intensity of the physical side of the experience was simply too magnificent.

It was then that I had my first break through.

It was like God silenced the wind and waves and began to speak. "Jeff, wake up. Do you really think that the Evil One is going to allow us to continue to take his territory without a fight?" I kept hearing that over and over again in my head until I finally fired back at God, "Wait a minute God! Aren't you supposed to protect me from stuff like this? Are you telling me this is from the Evil One?"

God fired back, "All sickness is from the Evil One, but I could remove it if I wanted to. Greater is He that is in you than he that is in the world, right? Do you believe this, Jeff?"

I was getting angry at this point. "Then, why don't You remove this? Are You going to sit idly by and let him do this thing to me?"

He replied, "My grace is sufficient for you."

For those of you freaking out right now, let me assure you this was not an audible conversation. However, that did not make it any less real. Furthermore, any voices you think you might hear should always be measured against the objective truth of God's Word. The trouble with the conversation I just had with God was that it was objectively tenable. It was consistent with what has already been revealed in His Word, the Bible. God never made a contract with me whereby He promised that no rain would ever come into my life. Actually, He promised the opposite. "In this world you will have trouble, but take heart, I have overcome the world" (John 16:33).

But there is another promise that is equally powerful and effective. God promised that He would take things that are meant for evil and use them for His good and perfect purpose in the world. Moreover, the Apostle Paul's thorn in the flesh reminds us that through all the rains we are called to endure, God's strength is made perfect in our weakness.

After months and months of tests, trials, and horrific, overwhelming, debilitating experiences, the light was beginning to shine bright. The rain that was coming into my life was for God's purposes. He was taking me from glory to glory and washing away the chaff and squeezing me until the bad stuff could be removed and the good stuff come out! Yes, the rains were about to make me into the man God had always intended me to become.

By now, those of you who have experienced these same symptoms are all too familiar with this illness. After months of echocardiograms, stress tests, and every other heart examination a man can have, the doctors determined that I was as healthy as a person could possibly be. No heart issues, no diabetes, no blood issues, no viruses. I was the poster boy of good health and vitality. But every time I heard a doctor tell me this, the frustration grew. I was relieved to hear that my heart was in good shape but frustrated beyond belief that no one could explain what was happening to me.

Finally, one day a friend of mine encouraged me to see a Psychiatrist. My first response was, "Are you crazy?" No pun intended. "Why would I see a Psychiatrist?"

He quickly responded, "Because perhaps your issue is not physical but mental."

When I heard that I wanted to belt him right between the eyes. However, the more I thought about it the more I was willing to consider that perhaps there was something to it. After all, I had gotten nowhere with general practitioners. Most of them wanted to pump heart medicines into me as sort of a trial and error to discover what was really wrong. Instead of getting better I was getting worse. In fact, at one point I was so devastated and confused that the thought of suicide entered my mind. I said the "thought." I never actually acted on it but began to have greater sympathy for people who had. The thought of living every single day for the rest of my life with these feelings of overwhelming anxiety was too much to consider. When my mind would begin going in that direction, I would stop the spinning by distracting myself with something that would capture my attention, like golf, or exercise, or Everybody Loves Raymond, my favorite television comedy.

So, with indescribable apprehension, I made an appointment with Dr. Jack Lindheimer in Pasadena. Although his office assistants could use a few lessons in personal relations and bedside manner, the doctor himself is knowledgeable, personal, and just flat out wicked smart!

From the first time I met him I was enthralled. Within minutes he diagnosed the problem and began to explain to me what was happening. It was a breath of fresh air. He knew the problem and solution. Within six weeks I was beginning to feel like the old Jeff Vines. I wanted to run, work out, eat out, see movies, go to Laker games, and play golf. Over the next months the rain began to subside. He had accurately diagnosed the problem. I was suffering from severe Anxiety Disorder.

Anxiety Disorder is a type of mental illness that affects more than 25 million Americans. The core symptom of panic disorder is the panic attack, an overwhelming combination of physical and psychological distress. During an attack several of these symptoms occur in combination: pounding heart or chest pain; sweating, trembling, shaking; shortness of breath, sensation of choking; nausea or abdominal pain; dizziness or lightheadedness; feeling unreal or disconnected; fear of losing control, "going crazy," or dying; numbness; chills or hot flashes.

Because symptoms are so severe, many people with panic disorder believe they are having a heart attack or other life-threatening illness. (For more information, check out the following website: http://www.psychiatry.org/anxiety-disorders).

Hearing this diagnosis was extremely difficult in some respects, relieving in others. Yes, I now knew that I had an actual medical condition. That was the good news. The bad news was that I was ignorant when it came to mental illnesses. In fact, I was often cold and indifferent to people who claimed they experienced depression, bi-polarism, anxiety or any other form of mental disease. I would listen and tell them I would pray for them but down deep inside I was thinking, "Dude, suck it up. We all go through times of sadness and depression and worry and doubt. Be a man! Bow your neck and show a little intestinal fortitude."

I never said this out loud, thank God, but I thought it more times than I would like to admit. But now here I was right smack dab in the middle of a mental illness that can be defined but not fully explained. The attacks still come but they are fewer, less intense and bearable. As I mentioned before, I do not believe God has taken them completely away for reasons I will further explain below.

For now however, it is important to clarify that "anxiety disorder" has very little to do with being anxious about anything. The medicines that cure or make bearable the attacks are not magic pills that make all your problems go away. They are medicines that simply balance serotonin levels in the brain. This is a chemical issue. Experiencing depression or anxiety can have very little to do with the fact you are sad or worried about something. Obviously, these issues can be part of the problem but are not necessarily part of the solution. Yes, you may be worried about paying the bills, anxious about your children's future, or even sad about the loss of someone you love, but, none of these things need to be present in order for you to experience depression or anxiety disorder.

Serotonin levels in the brain can have much to do with the way a person feels. Moreover, there are so many things that affect these levels—diet being a major contributor. I don't want to get into the foods and chemicals we are putting into our bodies but I will tell you this—eating right has greatly decreased the regularity and intensity of my anxiety attacks.

Diet may not be the cure-all but a good one certainly helps. Things like sugar and caffeine are major contributors to mental illness. Of this I am certain. I do not want to turn this into a medical lecture, but if you are interested in mental illness, causes, effects, and cures, I encourage you to talk to a respected psychiatrist (emphasis on respected). For our purposes, I want to focus on three important things.

First, I have no doubt that God sent this rainstorm into my life. For the theologians out there who may struggle with the way I worded that last line, I think it is important to remember that in the Hebrew mind every event came from God. They did not struggle with the issue of what was "caused" or what was "allowed" by God. The issue was that nothing ever happens in our world or in our lives that God could not have easily prevented. That is what it means for God to be sovereign.

Joseph understood this extremely well. His response to his brothers when they apologize for all the pain they had caused him was, "What you meant for evil, God used for good, the saving of the nation." This is a powerful historical statement that possesses deep theological and personal ramifications. There is simply no way around it, God takes the evil intentions of mankind and the debilitating impact of an ailing world inundated with sin and continues to achieve His grand purposes and designs.

Rainstorms are no problem for God. Sometimes they are not storms of correction. Joseph was not being punished for his sins, but storms of perfection, the prospering and refining of a nation.

The three years in which I suffered from severe anxiety attacks were the best three years of my life in some respects. Why? It was during those years that I began to know God in the way He seeks to be known. My intimacy with God during those days was unparalleled to those of days gone by. You will never know Jesus is all you need until Jesus is all you have. Only when we are so desperate and empty of self-sufficiency will we begin to turn to God and come back home to the only place of real hope and security.

There can be no doubt that when God wants to do a mighty work in us, He must first draw us toward a greater intimacy with Him in order that we may draw from His resources to accomplish the task. The major rainstorms of life are the very events that create in us a greater desire to be in the presence of God. He knows that. We know that. Yet, we still resist the rain.

Second, I could not help but remember my mother's prayer for me recorded in her journal that I found after her death. "I pray that Jeff will learn to love people and not use them as a means to an end." Every lead pastor, no matter the size of his church, small, medium, or mega, if he is honest, struggles with this issue. If we are not careful we begin building our kingdom rather than God's. When we begin building our own, people become nothing more than a means to an end. They are tools in our hands to build our monstrosities to ourselves in hopes that people will come from all around to see what we have made with our own two hands.

Once again, mom's prayer was having full impact in my life. For the first time in my life I was gaining a heart of empathy and concern for those who were suffering from mental illness. The harsh, judgmental, "suck it up" spirit that had dominated much of my life concerning this group of people was slowly fading and being replaced by tears.

Preaching six services every weekend can be grueling and there are often times I just want to go backstage and lay down on the couch and rest before time for the next sermon arrives. Yet, when someone struggling with mental illness approaches me, time seems to stand still. All my other concerns dissipate and the person has my full attention. Only God could cause such a transformation in me and only the rainstorm of personal struggles could accomplish it.

In fact, after hearing horror story after horror story of how Christians had been treated by other Christian friends after sharing their struggles with some mental illness, I became determined to use the platform God has given me to speak openly about my ongoing fight with my own illness. I want to remind people that God loves them and rather than cower from the rains, embrace them, allowing God to do His perfect work in us.

The first weekend I mentioned my illness there was an overwhelming shock (How could Pastor Jeff suffer from this? He is such a man of faith and he trusts in God. This does not seem possible). The shock was followed by immeasurable gratitude from those who were in the middle of a similar journey. To know that your senior pastor is struggling with the same heavy rains that are plaguing your life seemed to bring sweet relief to many.

Third, once I discovered the hundreds of people suffering from anxiety and depression I became more determined to help them weather their intimidating storms. This is where I had to tread very carefully. Even though mental illness is a real disease and is the result of so many different outside and inside agents, I have learned that God is still the only answer and ultimate cure. True, various medications can decrease the intensity of the symptoms, increasing one's ability to function with confidence, but ultimate healing comes through Jesus. Let me explain.

God is sovereign over every part of our physical make-up. He owns it all. To resist medicine is foolishness because God gifted men and women on planet earth to effectively deal with the issues we face, even those of our own doing. God is gratuitously gracious. He yearns for His people and will one day bring full and complete relief to every ailment known to man. Yet, even while we wait for what is yet to come, God, in His mercy, grants us knowledge of the human body and greater understanding of the physical, psychological, and physiological makeups.

When we seek to understand creation we seek to know the mind of God. This is precisely why much of what we know in the scientific world originated from the early Christians who did not see a conflict between science and faith. Science was meant to explain the "what" while theology was mean to explain the "why." When a person begins to understand the Psalmist when he wrote, "The earth is the Lord's and everything in it. He founded upon the seas and established it upon the waters (Psalm 24)," he will begin to understand all its implications. God, in His mercy grants us grace and mercy through the world of medicine but medicine only goes so far. Only God can make us whole.

When my "anxiety disorder" became overwhelming, those things in my life with which I had insufficiently dealt came to the surface. For example, I had not previously realized my great fear of death. Deep inside I knew my belief in Jesus and the power of the resurrection was strong. In fact, it was not death itself, the mere reality of my heart stopping and life on this earth coming to an end that frightened me so. No, instead, it was the impact my death would have on my wife and children and on my church. The thought that my children would have to grow up without their father terrified me. I wanted my daughter to have her father walk her down the aisle at her wedding. That's my job! I need to be there to do it! I knew my son needed his father to be there to coach him through the various storms he will encounter in dating, marriage, career and even his faith. That's part of what fathers are supposed to do and I did not want to let him down.

Through all of this I began to discover the limitations of my faith in God. After all, if God decided it was time for me to head home, was He not able to reveal His prevailing presence in the midst of every storm my wife and children may face? If God can take care of me in eternity can He not also watch over my children in the temporal? He is sovereign over life, death and everything in between.

The season in which I experienced my worst anxiety forced me to deal with my greatest fears and in doing so, with the power and knowledge of God, I was able to defeat them. I began to realize that the best thing I could do in the midst of all of the rainstorms was raise my spiritual umbrella and live under God's sovereign rule. Trusting in any and every circumstance would bring about a peace I had not previously known. That's what it means to live in the kingdom of God. "Do not be anxious for anything but by prayer and supplication make your requests known to God and the peace of God that passes all understanding will guard your hearts and minds in Christ Jesus" (Phil 4:6-7). Notice what is guarded or kept in perfect peace—our hearts (the seat of the emotions) and our minds (the seat of all our thoughts and fears).

Now here I am at fifty years old. Two things have happened: One, I am much more relaxed than I have ever been. Even when the anxiety attacks come I breathe my way through them (biofeedback) and see them no longer as foe but as friend —something to be embraced to allow God to complete His perfect work in me. What is absolutely amazing is that as soon as I do this, my brain seems convinced that I am not afraid, therefore, neither should my body exhibit the signs related to fear. So, the anxiety fades as quickly as it came. Don't misunderstand. I still don't like the rains, especially when they come at the most inconvenient times. However, God is Sovereign over the rain and He could stop the rain but often chooses not to. Therefore, I can only assume that this particular rainstorm must come into my life in order that the chaff be washed away, that my mother's prayer may be answered, and ultimately, that I will bear the fruit God intended on me producing from the foundations of the world.

I have continued with a much more wholesome diet and exercise routine. When I run I often find myself repeating the words, "God determines who lives or dies" in perfect timing with each foot hitting the ground before the next one strikes behind it. The anxiety attacks still come from time to time, but, through everything, God has revealed Himself yet again. There are many who choose to run from God into the distant land when these types of illnesses come. This is a mistake. You will never find the healing in a distant land. If you will run home to the Father, through patience, endurance, and a passion to seek and to know God, you will discover Him in a way you never thought possible. The rains may come but they just won't have the power they used to have, and, through each rainstorm God will reveal Himself to you in a deeper and more intimate way than you had previously known Him.

Okay, what about you? This is where the rubber hits the road! What chaff does God need to remove from your life. Here is the thing about chaff; its tough stuff! Chaff usually does not go without a fight. In fact, chaff will often disguise itself as wheat. Jesus warned us that only He was able to fully and truly distinguish between the two (Matthew 13). If you want to truly know God in the way He seeks to be known, you have to get down on your knees and ask Him to "reveal any wicked way in you." You have to give Him permission to rid you of all your idols, anything you place your dependence upon regarding your safety, security, significance and preservation other than God Himself.

Moreover, you have to pray that God would reveal anything about Himself that you do not yet know. Remember, truly knowing God brings huge dividends. Joy becomes central, sorrow only peripheral. Every time God reveals a deeper knowledge and understanding of Himself, something shallow and temporary is replaced by something deep and eternal.

When my daughter Sian was eight years old she developed severe asthma. We were living in New Zealand at the time and this beautiful country down under is also known for its high mold and mildew count. After all, a country that has on the average 282 days of rain per year is going to struggle with dampness, right? Sian's asthma got so bad that I began bargaining with God. "God please, for the umpteenth time, heal my daughter's disease. Please. If not, I don't see how we can remain in a place where my daughter's life is at risk. I know that you have sent us here to proclaim Your Name, to bind the brokenhearted and to set the captives free, so, can You please set this captive, Sian, free?"

Struggling day after day with this dilemma I spent time every night in her room praying that God would take away this debilitating physical ailment. At the same time New Zealand television was airing a commercial that featured a famous line, "When you can't breathe, nothing else matters." Every time I saw it I was reminded of the pain Sian was experiencing. If you've ever had severe asthma you know how frightening this disease can be. One night, after an hour or more of pleading with God to remove Sian's asthma, the Lord spoke to me again. I did not hear an audible voice but the message was no less clear. "Jeff, how I wished you were as much concerned with Sian's spiritual health as you are her physical."

I cannot tell you the impact that had on me. Suddenly, I began to realize the lack of serious effort exerted toward teaching my children the words of life. As if my eyes were opened for the first time, I began to see how I spent so much time teaching others that I failed to teach the one's God had entrusted to me. This life-defining moment changed everything. The next morning I went to the local Christian book store and purchased a copy of a book by John MacArthur entitled, *Faith to Grow On.* I had heard about this book from others but had made no real effort to track it down, until that day. This fantastic little book is theology and apologetics wrapped up into a child sensitive package that educates and inspires at the same time. I made a commitment to God and myself to pour into my children basic Bible doctrine, apologetics, and most importantly, my personal experiences with God. Both my children will graduate from Hope International University this year with degrees in International Business. Delaney and Sian will tell you that much of what they learned from me in the home served as the foundation upon which they would view and understand everything else.

This experience with Sian's asthma quite literally saved their spiritual lives. In fact, so many things changed after Sian's illness. Yes, God did indeed make her well. The doctors were amazed at how she quickly recovered and never struggled with Asthma again. However, the healing did not come until the message God wanted to send was received and obeyed. I needed a spiritual reawakening to my responsibilities as a father and a husband. I remember seeing the look on my wife's face the first time she walked into the kids bedroom to see all of us seated on the floor reading from *Faith to Grow On*, discussing the wonders of God and talking about the most important things in life.

In Sian's illness I met the God who speaks words of life and desires that those words be taught to our children for generations to come. I met the God who fills young Christian women with love toward husbands who diligently teach and train up their children in the way they should go so that when they are old they will not depart from Him. I met the God who is willing to allow pain and suffering into my life in order to turn my attention toward those things that truly matter. Finally, I met the God who heals. When Sian's asthma miraculously went away without any medical explanation, I knew from where the healing had come.

Please listen carefully. This is just one of the traumatic experiences I endured after my mother's death. They were many others. My son Delaney went through a season where he was bleeding internally and of course, as parents, you think Leukemia or some other devastating disease. Although my wife and I lost our first child in an automobile accident in Zimbabwe long before my mother's passing, I never really dealt with the pain until years later when I began to live the tragic experience all over again, questioning God's reasoning and the reality of ever seeing our son again. I could go on and on and on but, it was my own personal rainstorm that changed everything—especially the way I began to see God, tragedy, and the manner in which God reveals Himself to us.

When God Wants To Drill A Man

When God wants to drill a man,
And thrill a man,
And skill a man,
When God wants to mold a man
To play the noblest part;

When He yearns with all His heart
To create so great and bold a man
That all the world shall be amazed,
Watch His methods, watch His ways!

How He ruthlessly perfects
Whom He royally elects!
How He hammers him and hurts him,
And with mighty blows converts him

Into trial shapes of clay which
Only God understands;
While his tortured heart is crying
And he lifts beseeching hands!
How He bends but never breaks
When his good He undertakes;
How He uses whom He chooses,

And with mighty power infuses him;
By every act induces him
To try His splendor out
God knows what He's about.

– Anonymous

CHAPTER 8

Knowing God: Where It All Really Begins

John 21 is an amazing chapter in the Bible. The chapter itself is actually an addendum to the book of John. The historical life of Jesus is recorded in the previous twenty chapters. Jesus' teaching ministry, miracles, life, death, burial, and resurrection have all been described and celebrated. The disciples have seen Jesus. Thomas has doubted and Judas has betrayed Jesus. End of story, right? Wrong.

For some reason John feels compelled to add one more chapter to his account. He wants to answer a question he knows will be on the hearts and minds of his readers: whatever happened to Peter? The last his readers had heard about Peter was that he had denied even knowing Jesus. The one who said, "Even if all these other disciples leave you, I will never forsake you Jesus," left Jesus high and dry when Jesus needed him most. So what happened to Peter and Jesus? Did Jesus confront Peter? Was there ever an intervention? Did the other disciples say to their leader, Peter, "Dude, you gotta stop over-promising and under-delivering." I believe John includes his twenty-first chapter to not only deal with the question of Jesus' and Peter's relationship but to remind us today what it is that Jesus wants most from us. Its not our money nor our sacrifice. Its something far more valuable of which these things become the natural by-products.

As the chapter opens we find Peter and the other disciples standing by the Sea of Tiberias (Gallilee) as commanded by Jesus, waiting on further instructions from the Savior Himself. Every time the disciples are listed by name as they are in verse 2, Peter's name appears first. Why? Because he is the leader of the twelve. Suddenly, in verse 3, Peter says, "I am going fishing." Whats interesting is that the manner in which this verse is written suggests that Peter is not merely going on a fishing excursion on this particular day, but is instead returning to his old occupation as a fisherman for good.

Think about it for a moment. In Peter's mind he has been an absolute disaster as a disciple. On one occasion he actually rebuked Jesus for suggesting that He was sent into the world to die. Jesus actually responded to Peter by saying, "Get thee behind me Satan." Then of course there is this whole thing about denial. At any rate, Peter probably thinks he is irredeemable and the best thing he could do for all involved is simply go back to what he knows best, fishing.

So he disobeys a direct order from Jesus to stay by the Sea of Galilee, gets into a boat and goes back to his old occupation. Worse yet, the other disciples say, "We'll go with you" (21:3). What happens next is astounding. They fish all night and catch nothing. Then, as morning arrives, Jesus stands on the shore and shouts to them, "Friends, do you have any fish?" (21:5). The disciples shouted back, "No." Then Jesus responded, "Throw your net on the right side of the boat and you will find some (21:5b-6)." The rest is history. They caught so many fish that they were unable to haul the net (obviously for fear the net would break and they would lose all the fish).

Have you noticed something? This encounter with the disciples mirrors the very first encounter Jesus had with Peter in Luke 5 when Peter had been fishing all night and had caught nothing until Jesus appeared and asked him to put the nets out into the deep at which point the fish came rolling in (Luke 5:6). Back in John 21, as soon as the nets are filled with fish Peter experiences a dejavu, recognizes Jesus and begins sprinting toward the shore to greet Him. But somewhere between the boat, the water and the shore, Peter relented. What happened? Did Peter suddenly remember his denial and the embarrassment of being confronted by Jesus on this matter and this caused a reluctance to meet the Savior? Did the thought cross his mind that he really isn't that good of a fisherman either and without Jesus, he would be lost at sea without compass or sail? Or maybe it was something far more simple and far more important that caused Peter to shrink from a face-to-face encounter.

Perhaps when Jesus recreated the original scene of Peter's calling to be a fisher of men, Peter remembered the commitment he had made with Jesus and how once again, by returning to the open sea as a fisherman, he had not kept his word.

Regardless of the circumstances, Peter suddenly is quiet while the other disciples celebrate the magnitude of their catch by actually counting the number of fish, 153 to be exact.

After breakfast, Jesus decides its time for an intervention. He takes Peter aside and asks him a simple question, "Peter, do you love me more than these (John 21:15)?" Whether Jesus meant more than the disciples or more than the fish is unclear. Perhaps Jesus was reminding Peter of his "although all the other disciples will forsake you, I will never leave you" statement. "You said you would love me more than the other disciples and yet you denied even knowing me." Perhaps Jesus was reminding Peter that he had already left his previous occupation when he answered Jesus call to be a fisher of men. Why had he changed his mind and returned to what he had previously known. Whatever "these" represents, Peter was quick to the draw and categorically states, "Yes Lord, you know that I love you" (21:15).

This particular passage is one that is difficult to translate into English. What is not seen is the fact that when Jesus asks Peter if he loves Him, Jesus uses the word, *Agapao* or *Agape,* which means "unconditional love." Yet, when Peter responds, "Yes, Lord, I love you," he does not use the word *"agapao"* but instead *"phileo,"* a word used to describe friendship. There are in fact four popular words translated "love" in the New Testament. *Agape,* the highest most lofty love is a word that refers to the unconditionality of God's love for us. *Storge,* a parental type of love is used to describe the love a mother has for her children. *Phileo,* a friendship type of love is used to describe the love between two friends, and, finally, *Eros,* an erotic type of love is used to describe the relationship between two lovers.

When Jesus asks Peter if he loves Him with an unconditional agape-type love, Peter responds, "Yes, Lord, you know that You and I are best buddies." Why does he do that? Because Peter knows he cannot claim the highest love. Unconditional love would not have included denying he even knew Jesus at a time when Jesus needed Peter's love so desperately. So, Peter responds accordingly. However, Jesus is not going to let Peter off the hook so easily. He asks him a second time, "Peter, do you love (*agape*) me?" Peter responds again, "Yes, Lord, I love you." Once again Peter avoids *agape* (unconditional love) and employs *phileo* (friendship love). For a second time Jesus commands Peter to "feed my sheep" (16b). Not satisfied with leaving things as they are, Jesus asks Peter one final time, "Simon, do you love me" (21:17)?

Interestingly, this time Jesus uses Peter's own word, *phileo*, questioning even Peter's friendship type of love. At this Peter is disheartened. In fact, Peter is grieved at the fact that Jesus would question his friendship. So he responds by saying, "Lord, you know all things; you know that I love you" (21:17b,c). Peter makes a statement of omniscience. Peter is asking the God of the universe to use his transcendent power to look past Peter's fleshly failures deep into his heart and find the love that Peter truly feels for Jesus. Jesus responds by simply saying, "Feed my sheep."

This is the most important question Jesus asks His followers. Do you love Me more than anything else. Why does He ask? Because what we love ultimately we pursue most passionately. What we truly love, we pursue. What we truly love most, we pursue most. Any lesser love gets sacrificed for the sake of our highest love.

Retuning to the dating analogy, I remember when Robin and I were first dating. There is nothing I would not sacrifice for her. I mean, I was really something before the marriage ceremony. I would sacrifice Monday Night Football just to take long walks with her. I would miss playing basketball with my buddies just to take Robin to dinner and engage in meaningful conversation. I would even sacrifice going to the movies or buying fast food just so I could save enough money to buy her roses that would last three of four days at the most. Why? Because what you love you pursue, and, what you love ultimately, you sacrifice ultimately for.

Jesus confronts Peter with the idea of unconditional love because He wants to remind Peter that that is the only type of love God is interested in. We can have other loves and other pursuits but our highest love and ultimate pursuit must be Jesus or we will never know God in the way He seeks to be known. Let's go back to what we have said before. What is the real problem with the trials of our lives? We love safety and convenience more than the pursuit of the knowledge of God. You say, "That's unfair Jeff. I don't love convenience more than God. I just think God has the power to keep me safe from anything harmful." Well, you are correct. But the thing you are forgetting and most often are unwilling to admit is that God has our greatest and most intense attention when things are not going well in our lives. If we love money and security more than God, when these things are removed from us we will respond one of two ways. One, we will become angry with the Father and choose to live in a distant land, hoping to find safety, security and ultimate freedom apart from the Father or, two, we will run to God, choose to stay at home with the Father, looking to know Him in a way we had not previously known. There is simply no way around it. Jesus will not be able to take you where He wants you to go until you make up your mind whether or not you love Him "more than these"—more than anything else. Case in point: Peter. After Jesus pushes Peter to admit that his love for Jesus is still lacking, Jesus drops the hammer explaining why it is so crucial that Jesus becomes Peter's highest love.

> Very truly I tell you, when you were younger you dressed yourself and went where you wanted; but when you are old you will stretch out your hands, and someone else will dress you and lead you where you do not want to go." Jesus said this to indicate the kind of death by which Peter would glorify God. John 21:18-19

The phrase, "stretch out your hands" is used in extra-biblical literature as an expression signifying crucifixion. Jesus metaphorically places His arm around Peter and says, "Peter, right now you get up every morning and go wherever you want to go. Presently, you go where you want to go and do what you want to do. But Peter, the day is coming when someone else will wake you up at a time you would rather sleep. Someone else will dress you in clothing that you would rather not wear. Peter, just as they led me to Golgotha, they are going to take you to a place you would rather not go, and Peter, they will crucify you there, just as they did me.

Imagine hearing this for the first time. Peter knows who Jesus is. What Jesus says goes. He is God in the flesh, and, here He is telling Peter that he is going to die a horrible death and by this death God would be glorified. Any theology that does not include suffering for God's ultimate glory or gain is utterly destroyed by this narrative. Jesus is not merely asking Peter if he loves Him more than anything else in this life. He is asking Peter if he loves Jesus more than life itself. When the time comes that Jesus asks Peter to die for Him, is Peter's love so strong that he is willing to sacrifice all lesser loves for the sake of Christ's kingdom? Even his very own life?

This is precisely why Jesus confronted Peter with the order of his loves. Only if Peter truly loved Jesus more than anything else would he be willing to give everything else away for the sake of the Savior.

The story is told of a king and a slave. The king's daily routine took him by the mud pit in which the slave tirelessly and happily worked. One day the king dismounted from his horse, peeked over the side of the pit and said to the slave, "Slave, I don't quite understand you. Every day I pass by this miserable pit to find you whistling, happily and joyfully working in the mud. I don't get it. From where do you find such joy?" The slave responded, "Get your white suit on, come down into the mud, and I will show you." To which the King responded, "Oh no, I can't do that," and moved on. This scenario was repeated day after day for months with the slave responding to the King's question, "Where can I find your joy" with the words, "Get your white suit on, come down into the mud, and I will show you." Finally, the King said to the servant, "Ok, I'll do it!" at which point the slave said, "No king, you don't have to; you only need to be willing."

The truth is that Jesus will probably not ask most of you reading this book to die for the cause of Christ. But He does need to know that you would be willing to do so if He so required. When you think of such a scenario where does your mind go? In fact, what is the one thing you would be unwilling to give up for the cause of Christ? That thing is your true idol—the thing that you simply cannot live without. When God becomes the one thing you truly cannot live without, then and only then, will you stop going so hard after your lesser loves and begin to pursue God with the type of passion that would give up everything to know His glory and to glorify Him.

In Chuck Colson's book, *Knowing God*, Colson tells the story of Telemekus, a fourth century Asiatic monk who lived among the recluse of his private gardens. Unwilling to be tainted by the world, Telemekus spent hours in morning prayer pursuing the knowledge of God and, as a result learned to discern the voice of God in all matters. One day while Telemekus was praying he heard the voice of the Lord commanding him to leave his place of refuge in the mountains in order to descend upon the people in the city below for a purpose that would later be revealed to him. Heeding the voice of his master, he readied himself for the jounrey and set out for the hustle and bustle of city life.

When he arrived just inside the city gates a large crowd also descended capturing the old monk and thrusting him into the middle of the area where the gladiator games were about to begin. Of course, as one who had not yet been desensitized to the blood and gore of such games, Telemekus found these events offensive and hellish. As the victims were being torn apart by wild animals for the entertainment of the masses, Telemekus stood up and exclaimed, "In the name of Jesus Christ, stop this thing!"

Due to the deafening noise of the boisterous crowd, the monk's pleas remained unheard and unheeded. Not discouraged, Telemekus ran down onto the killing fields and screamed, "In the name of Jesus Christ, stop this thing! Forbear!" Gaining both the attention and anger of the crowd, Telemekus shouted again, "In the name of Jesus, stop this thing!" At that point the crowd began to shout to the guards, "Run him through! Run him through!" The guards obliged the crowd and with a sword running through his torso and the crowd silencing their pleas, the faithful monk shouted one more time, "Please, in the name of Jesus Christ, stop this thing." One by one the crowd began to exit the arena and although many other things were brought to bear, never again was there a fight in the gladiatorial arena. Through one faithful, obedient man who had grown to know, truly know, the living God, the world changed for the good and for the cause of Christ.

Perhaps the most defining mark of a person who is progressing in their knowledge of God is this: they become less about self and more about others and even more so about the kingdom of God. I meet with pastors all over the world who are frustrated that they can't get more of a commitment out of their congregational members. They have tried everything under the sun. Giving campaigns, service opportunities, evangelism crusades and the like. These may work for a season but they will never create genuine commitment to Christ and His cause. The lack of commitment to the work of Jesus is a symptom of a greater disease. Our people don't know Jesus because we have not shown them what He is truly like. My job as a pastor in not to manipulate, guilt, and coerce people into giving their lives away but to show and give them Jesus that He may transform them from the inside out. When you come to know Jesus as He truly is you can't help but experience total transformation. Our people and our churches are shallow because we are not spending time with Jesus, or, if we are, it's out of some duty we feel or religious ritual that we don't feel at all. Until we love Jesus more than anything else we will not be willing to sacrifice everything for Him and we will most definitely not be willing to go wherever He leads us.

After informing Peter of his impending death, Jesus turns to Peter and says, "Follow Me." Again, in the original language it appears as if Jesus demonstrates for Peter what He is demanding that Peter do, follow Him as He begins to walk. Before Peter even takes the first step of obedience toward Jesus, he evidently turns to John and says, "What about this dude?" In other words, "If I have to die for your sake, what about John? Does he get off scott free?" Jesus response is classic, "If I want him to remain alive until I return, what is that to you?" In other words, "Peter, that's none of your business. Stop worrying about everybody else and do what I ask you to do. Follow Me" (21:22).

Here's the rub. No two lives are ever the same. Where Jesus leads one He may not lead another. Why? Because every event of every life is designed by God to encourage Divine Romance. God knows exactly where He has to lead us to compel us into relationship with Him. Moreover, He knows the paths our lives must take in order that He may reveal a part of Himself we had not previously known. Just as the path of effective courtship is not the same for every young girl, so also are there differences between what may draw me toward God and what may draw you toward God. Furthermore, because each of us has a specific calling on our lives, there will be some aspect of the nature of God that will be essential for you to learn in order for you to effectively accomplish your calling while other aspects of God's nature may be necessary for me to achieve mine. Lives take different paths because all lives are fearfully and wonderfully made (Psalm 139). The life that dies to self and lives for God is the life that finds both the real authentic self and the real authentic God. There is no other way.

CHAPTER 9

He's Still Waiting

We often assume that we have the right to rainy-free lives. Somewhere along the line we began to believe that no rain should ever come our way. Why? Most people I meet can never answer that question. On what basis do you believe that no rain should ever come into your life? Because you are a good person? Because you have never done anything wrong? Wow! Talk about overestimating one's own goodness! If those who live good lives deserve shelter from all potential rain, then would anyone qualify? Moreover, where is the cut line? Who makes the cut? How good is good enough? Every time we do something wrong should we experience a little rain? Should the measure of rain fit the magnitude of the failure. Perhaps we need some serious introspection concerning the goodness of God and the lack of goodness in us. Then, when the rain comes, we will react differently to it.

❖ ❖ ❖ ❖ ❖ ❖ ❖ ❖ ❖

On June 3rd, 2009 the town of Greensboro, North Carolina received four inches of rain in just two hours. All of the city's lakes, streams, and rivers overflowed, shutting down many of the roads. The local television and radio stations were warning people not to go outside because the situation was so dangerous.

A fifty year-old woman who had lost her license to a DUI decided she was going to drive her moped despite the terrible flooding and media warnings (in North Carolina you don't need a license to drive a moped).

She drove through a police roadblock—she saw it but thought she could make it—and was quickly washed off the road and into the river that it paralleled. A police officer threw a rope in for her and after a long struggle he was finally able to pull her out of the river.

After ensuring that the woman was alright the policeman went over to his patrol car to report to the dispatcher what had just happened. When he turned around to check on the woman he discovered that she had jumped back in for a second time, a 'double dip.'

What goes through a person's mind to make them do something like that? What was the thought process, sequentially, that led this woman to do such a thing? How did she reach the conclusion that the best thing to do in her current circumstance was to jump back in the water? What you believe determines what you do. Something in this woman's belief system made her jump back in. Maybe she did it because she didn't want to lose her moped. Maybe she thought she was a strong enough swimmer, or that she would float, or that the courageous, good-looking policeman would save her again, or maybe she thought that she could ride the moped out of the torrent. I don't know what she was thinking; all I can tell you is that it was wrong because she drowned!

What you believe matters because it determines how you live. If you believe that money grows on trees you're probably going to plant at least a few trees in your yard, right? If you believe that aliens come down and abduct people during full moons you're likely to stay inside around the time of the full moon. If you believe that by eating chocolate you'll have a pimple-fest on your face you're almost certainly going to limit how much chocolate you eat, if not avoid it entirely. This isn't a problem until what you believe is wrong, because then your wrong beliefs can lead to wrong activity.

Go back to the moped lady—I don't know what she was thinking but it was erroneous and she died! What you believe matters because it determines how you live. Jesus has to change a major belief in every single one of us. This wrong belief in us is producing wrong activity. It's a belief so natural that it's as intuitive and instinctive as eating and sleeping. It's ingrained in human nature. This belief is producing wrong activity in your life, and that wrong activity is robbing you of joy and peace and everything good that God wants you to have.

When God wants to change a fundamental belief system in us it's not going to be easy because this is a major belief that is in every one of us. It's so innate, it's intrinsic. It's instinctive and natural to think this way. He can't change this belief just by simply dispensing information and rationalizing with us because we naturally resist change and get defensive. We even run away from it. Jesus, like all good teachers, does not give us a direct answer. He doesn't lecture us and list all the things we do and believe that are wrong. Instead, He takes a less confrontational approach—He asks us questions so that we see the assumptions within our beliefs, because all of our beliefs have underlying assumptions, and not all of these assumptions are correct.

WHY DO BAD THINGS HAPPEN TO GOOD PEOPLE?

In Luke 13 Jesus reminds His audience of a first century disaster that happened at Siloam. There was a tower under construction that collapsed. We are not told why, but it caved in and killed eighteen people. Jesus confronted those in the crowd, because he knew what they were thinking—that those people died because of the bad things they had done. We can be guilty of the same thing—we often think that disasters happen to bad people or people who've done bad things. In Luke 13:4a Jesus says, "Do you think they were more guilty than all the others living in Jerusalem? I tell you, no! But unless you repent you too will all perish" (NIV).

When any tragedy occurs these kinds of questions begin to come. After the September 11th attacks many people in America started wondering if God was judging our country or if He had turned His back on us. I watched interview after interview on CNN and Fox in the days and weeks after the tragedy as the interviewers questioned evangelical after evangelical as to why God allowed this to happen. Billy Graham's wife, Ruth was interviewed by Fox and she said, "Well, we told God to get out of the classroom, get out of our lives, get out of our culture, and get out of our nation, and maybe God just heard us and listened and removed His hand of protection from our county."

I'm not saying that what she said was right or wrong, but I was amazed at how aggressively they came after her for that statement. Even the conservative media thought that was a preposterous idea.

What was even more interesting in the interviews were some of the other questions that were asked. Questions like, "why were some people spared while other people died?" After the tragedy many people who worked in the towers said that they had a feeling that they shouldn't go to the office that day. So, why didn't God give that intuition to everybody? Why did some people die while others lived? Those are the sorts of questions we all ask when something tragic happens. Are we spared because we are better people? Is it because those who suffered are more evil than us or they're worse sinners than we are?

When something bad happens to us our natural response is to wonder what we've done wrong, that maybe we're being punished by God or that we're just a bad person. The opposite is also in effect—when something good happens we tend to infer that it's because we're better than everybody else.

But Jesus is telling us that we have it all wrong. We need to change our assumptions and gain a new perspective that's counter-intuitive. Back in Luke 13, were those who were killed bad people and is that why the disaster happened to them? Jesus clearly says no. I like that answer; they're not worse than you. But it's the second part of this verse that I don't like, "…unless you repent you too will all perish" (Luke 13:5b, *NIV*).

He's not saying that we're good people and they're good people and it's just a random series of unfortunate events that can happen to anybody. What makes this passage so difficult is that Jesus is saying when it comes right down to it, every single one of us deserves to have a tower fall on us. In other words, what happened to them should have happened to you, so repent before a tower falls on you too! This begs the question: what erroneous intrinsic belief is Jesus trying to counter in our lives?

Over the course of my life I must have read fifteen books that ask, "Why do bad things happen to good people?" That makes me want to ask:

✦ Do bad people deserve bad things?

✦ Are you a good person?

✦ Do good people deserve good things?

✦ Are most people good or bad?

✦ How many good things do good people deserve?

The basic assumption behind that title is really bad philosophy—that there are some genocidal maniacs out there that deserve to have a tower on them but most of us don't! The assumption is that God owes you a good life.

Remember that a good teacher doesn't give you a straight answer when you ask a difficult question. Rather, they ask you other questions so that you see the assumptions within your original question. So, what are the philosophical assumptions behind the bad things/good people question? The first assumption is that most of us are good and do not deserve those bad things, but there are bad people out there that do. It also assumes that God owes us a good life and that up to this point our life has not been that great.

Jesus challenges us in Luke 13 to prove those assumptions. On what basis do you believe that God owes you a good life? Why do you think that your life isn't good right now? Think about it: God gives you life as a gift. Your breath is a gift—you didn't earn it. And it's not as if you did something in eternity past before you were born that was so good that it merited you being born. Being born is a gift. God grants you privileges that you did not and could not earn. The love between a man and a wife, family, relationships, nature, sunrise, sunset, sex within the context of marriage, and food that tastes good, not just sustenance. God could have just made food to give you energy, but instead He gave you the tongue, the palate, and taste—chocolate, blueberry pie, and cheesecake.

There are two experiences I remember in my life that stand out in this context. The first is my honeymoon—but not for the reason that you think! I remember three days after the wedding standing on the shore down in Jekyll Island, Georgia. My wife loves to swim and she was out in the ocean swimming with the dolphins. That moment overwhelmed me because I have been enamored with the beauty of my wife since day one, and I still am. I looked at her and thought, how on earth did I get this amazing woman? Who determined that marriage would be part of the human experience, that love should be part of life and that this beautiful woman would marry me? What did I do to earn that? Now even after twenty-six years of marriage I still wonder why I get to have this wonderful woman share a life and family with me.

A similar thought hit me when I was in Zimbabwe and saw Victoria Falls for the first time. I walked through the mist and made my way down the steps with a camera over my shoulder. I looked out and saw the great divide between Zambia and Zimbabwe into which the great Zambezi River falls and seems to stretch out forever. I thought, "Why do I get to experience this? Why don't I automatically bend my knee and give gratitude and worship to God? Why?" Because it's not innate. It's not an intrinsic response.

MORE ENJOYMENT, MORE DEMAND,
MORE ENTITLEMENT . . . LESS APPRECIATION

It was G.K. Chesterton who said, "Here dies another day during which I have had eyes, ears, hands and the great world around me; and with tomorrow begins another. Why am I allowed two?"

So often we have difficulty tearing ourselves away from our own self-indulgences. Sometimes it's difficult to get motivated to worship God. Studies show that the average church attendee comes once or twice a month for one service. That's one hour, maybe two. People tell me they don't read the Bible, or pray, or grow in their relationship with God because they don't have time. But surely we have more than two hours a month that we can give to God!

In Luke 13 Jesus says that we treat God with such great disdain, yet He's the giver of all good things and for some reason we truly believe that we deserve more. He gives so much to us, yet we don't worship and we're ungrateful and we truly believe He owes us more!

Gary Thomas, one of my favorite authors, wrote about taking his six year-old daughter Kelsey to Knott's Berry Farm. There were virtually no lines; they were having the time of their lives going from one ride to the next without having to wait. Little bumper cars, a train ride, a flying school bus, a Ferris Wheel, a log ride, they were riding on everything. He kept waiting for his little girl to come over and thank him for this great experience but instead, with a slightly desperate edge in her voice she said, "Daddy, what's next?"

As our enjoyment grows our demand grows. If we have something we like we generally want more of it. As our demand grows our entitlement grows. We think that because we had it before we deserve to have it again. Finally, as our entitlement grows our appreciation fades. We don't show any gratitude for the things that we think we deserve or to which we are entitled.

A few years ago I took my father-in-law and brother-in-law to play golf at my favorite golf course, Desert Dunes. I had been telling them for months that the best thing about this golf course was not the greens or the fairways, or the tee boxes or the traps. It was the hot dogs. They have really great hot dogs. Imagine how I must have felt when we got to the golf course and discovered that they had failed to renew their food license. That meant that the course was open but they had to shut down the concession stand. When I walked up to the counter and asked for three hot dogs with everything on them, the lady on the other side said, "Sorry sir, we don't have them."

If you could have seen the look on my face—it was the look that said, "You owe me a hotdog. I drove all the way out here and I told my family about your hot dogs. I demand a hotdog right now! Go get them, find me some, and bring them here. We're going to go play nine holes, and when we come back in I want my hotdogs!"

I didn't actually say any of that, but it's what I was thinking. As our enjoyment grows our demand grows, as our demand grows our entitlement grows, and as our entitlement grows our appreciation fades. We don't show gratitude for something we think is owed to us. We don't go in to our boss and say, "Thank you so much for my paycheck. You're a good man of grace and mercy. Thank you so much." No, more often our thought process goes more like this: "Give me my paycheck because I've earned every penny of it!"

When we think something is owed to us there is little or no gratitude. We live life with a constant "what's next" attitude—and we never give thanks in the moment.

In a documentary entitled *Wild Man Blues*, Woody Allen confessed, "I've got the kind of personality that when I'm here in Europe I miss New York and when I'm in New York I miss Europe. I just don't want to be where I am at any given moment. I would rather be somewhere else." There's no way to solve that problem because no matter where you are you will have chronic dissatisfaction—a problem I think many people have today. It doesn't just happen in Hollywood—everyone is susceptible to the entitlement attitude.

I've become enamored with the story of the professional basketball player Scottie Pippin over the last fifteen years. Pippin took a back seat to Michael Jordan until Jordan retired. Pippin was born into extreme poverty. His family was one of several families living in a one-room house. But in contrast, by 1999 Pippin signed a contract worth $14.7 million a year for three years. Add the commercial endorsements and he made $50 million dollars. It just went up from there. He owned a 74 foot yacht and a hundred thousand dollar Mercedes. He was living the life and yet he still wanted more.

An article was written about Pippin entitled "No Babe in the Woods" in the December 1999 issue of *Sports Illustrated*. The reporter asked Pippin what he thought about during pre-game warm-ups, and this was what the reporter recorded about the conversation:

> …Before every game in Portland's Rose Garden, Pippen only
> has eyes for one. He'll let his gaze drift over to the courtside seat

occupied by Paul Allen; cofounder of Microsoft and owner of both the Trail Blazers and the Seattle Seahawks, a man with a personal net worth of $40 billion. Pippen looks at his employer's geeky exterior and wonders...how does he do it... "What does he have? Forty billion? I want to know how: How can I make a billion? I just want one of them! What do I need to do...tell me how I can become a billionaire.

When I heard that I thought he needed to chill out! He already had $50 million, isn't that enough?

It reminded me of another professional athlete—this one a baseball player who was making $26 million. He felt that wasn't good enough so he went into arbitration with the team, asking for $68 million. They settled at a mere $52 million.

When they interviewed his wife after the arbitration and asked her how she felt she said, "it was the saddest day of our lives!" We have chronic disappointment, chronic complaining, and chronic dissatisfaction.

I go after husbands all the time but allow me to direct some thoughts to the wives reading these words. For some of you ladies your husbands are never going to be able to make you happy because you want more and more and he can never give you enough. Men have a deep desire for honor and want to provide for their wives and families; it's hard-wired in their DNA. When your husband knows he can't satisfy all your desires it robs him of his manhood because he knows he can never give you everything you need to make you happy.

Jesus said it's hard for a rich man to go to heaven. Before you just cast that aside, think about who's rich. When Jesus made this statement to be wealthy was to have more than a little hut and one meal a day. So if you're over and above that, you're rich! That definition makes almost everyone in America very wealthy. According to the United Nations, to be in the top 10% of the world's wealthiest only requires $61,000 in assets—a total of cash income, bank and investment accounts, and overall worth of material possessions such as cars and home. However, a recent magazine survey asked American men how much money they would need to have in their bank accounts before they would consider themselves to be rich. Over 74% said they would have to have at least one million dollars!

We're so affluent that it's hard for us to give thanks. When you're rich you only think about what you don't have instead of giving thanks and gratitude for what you do have. Because of our affluence there's seldom a reaching out for God. It's not just a problem in America, by the way. Another example is New Zealand—one out of every four kiwis owns a boat and the vast majority own a house on the beach. Every Friday at five o'clock everyone's gone for the weekend. God gets no time because they are so distracted by His blessings.

Consider the tension that must exist in the character of God. He looks down at us and says, "I love you. I love all my children, and there's so much I want to give you! But Jeff, if I give you that new set of golf clubs your heart desires, it's going to distract you. You're going to want to play more golf and that's not why I put you on the earth. So in this case I am going to have to say no."

That's exactly what happened to the children of Israel. God gave them the Promised Land and he said to Moses, "I'm concerned about My people because they're going to be harvesting where they have not planted and inheriting where they have not toiled and reaping where they have not sown. I am afraid that they will forget the Lord their God, by whose mercy all these gifts have come. So I want you to gather them together and I want you to tell them that I'm concerned about them, that they are going to forget Me."

We have our three square meals a day (sometimes four), we build our houses, buy nice clothes, and toys, and cars, and we're so wealthy in America that we even have little houses for our cars. God's concerned that when we've acquired all those material possessions we'll forget Him, that we will think that our power and the strength of our hands have produced wealth for us. Sure enough, that's exactly what happened to the Israelites, so much so that God compares the people He loves with a vineyard, and He says, "What more could I have done for my vineyard that I have done for it but yet I look for good grapes and I have found none."

What would it take to make you happy? Think about it: what do you need to finally reach a point where you have enough? I guarantee that your answer is drastically different than the answer that my friends in Zimbabwe give when I ask them the same question. They say that if they just had a mud hut with a roof that didn't leak and one meal a day that they would be happy. That's all they want. Why the huge discrepancy? Comparison. In our affluence we look around at what everyone else has and we say, "I want that too, and that too, and that too."

But in Zimbabwe there is no "that too." There's just not enough "that too" to go around, only the very basics of life.

When I walked into a tent to preach this message in Zimbabwe, there were people who flooded in from everywhere, they walked miles just to come and worship and praise God. The energy in that tent was unbelievable. People standing up with their hands in the air praising God just because they had a good rainy season and they grew a good crop of corn maize. Now that's true gratitude worship!

But when you're as rich as we are here in America, God's gifts never seem to be enough, because our eyes are always on what we don't have. Jesus says, "Repent lest ye likewise perish." Your attitude toward life is, "Why do bad things happen to good people?" Or, "Why is there so much pain and suffering in our world?" But Jesus said his philosophy is "Why does God allow so little pain given the fact that we treat Him with such disdain and no appreciation or gratitude?"

ONE MORE YEAR . . .

Jesus continues His teaching in Luke 13 by using a parable:

A man had a fig tree, planted in his vineyard, and he went to look for fruit on it, but did not find any. So he said to the man who took care of the vineyard, 'For three years now I've been coming to look for fruit on this fig tree and haven't found any. Cut it down! Why should it use up the soil?' 'Sir,' the man replied, 'leave it alone for one more year, and I'll dig around it and fertilize it. If it bears fruit next year, fine! If not, then cut it down' (Luke 13:6-9, *NIV*).

Let me illustrate what's happening here with a personal illustration. When we lived in New Zealand my wife and my daughter started batting those beautiful blue eyes at me, and asking, "Can we please get a puppy? Please, please, please?" Well of course I'm a softie and couldn't say no, so we got a puppy. But I set the ground rules—the man of the house puts his foot down. I said, "Ok, we can have a puppy but it has to be an outside dog only."

Two weeks went by, "Ok, the dog can be inside but only in the basement." I said.

Another two weeks went by, "Ok, the dog can come upstairs but only in Sian's room."

And then, "Ok, the dog can be in our room, but never on the bed."

And then, "Ok, the dog can be on the bed but never on my side." I said.

Then one day I came home after a long business trip and the dog was right there on my side of the bed hanging out with my wife. My wife Robin was incredibly patient with me until I came around to having our dog Milo. Now not only do I have a dog, but I also have a fish, a horse, and an ugly iguana terrorizing me at every moment of the day. I put my foot down, but Robin was patient.

This fig tree parable is beautiful because it's about a patient God. It's astounding when you think about it because here's what Jesus is saying to you and me: "I know what you're like. I know you don't give Me the honor due Me. I know you sometimes consider it a hassle to stop and bend your knee and worship. But the truth is that I love you and I just can't help myself. I love you despite your selfishness and sense of entitlement. I'm holding out for the possibility that you're going to change, that one day you're going to have a paradigm shift and you're going to begin to realize who I am and who you are and that nothing is owed to you and that you have so much and you'll start focusing on that and what you do have rather than what you do not have. And when you do there will be a peace that will flood your soul. It will come in like a cool summer breeze and you're going to be at peace with yourself, and you're going to be able to walk by the sea and just soak it in and enjoy that moment and not always be waiting for the next. You're going to be looking at the stars at night—the vastness. You're going to appreciate the love of your wife even it its imperfection, your children, and even everything you think that is wrong with your life and be able to say that at least you have it-- it may not be perfect but at least you have it."

One of my favorite memories growing up in east Tennessee was playing baseball with my brothers in the hot summer time. We played all day, only stopping when my mother brought us that sweet strawberry Kool-Aid. We would play until the last moment of light and then my mom would always come out and yell, "Come in boys, it's dark out there, time to come in, somebody's going to get hurt!"

We'd look over at mom and say, "Just one more pitch mom, just one more pitch!" Now what we really meant was 50,000 more pitches, but it just got her to let us play a little longer.

This parable is about Jesus going to God the Father who's the gardener and saying, "No, don't cut him down, just one more year God, just one more year. They're going to repent I know they are. Let me just dig around a bit and do some gardening, let me get out the pruning shears and hopefully I won't have to prune them too severely before they realize that they should have gratitude for even the simple basics of life." What He really means is 50,000 more years—"One more year God, just one more year."

One of my favorite movies is *Saving Private Ryan*, directed by Steven Spielberg.

I don't usually see movies like that but I went to see this one because I kept reading the reviews and thought it would give me a greater appreciation for those men and women who have served in our armed forces. The first twenty minutes were so intense, when they were trying to take the beach and just getting slaughtered in the boats and in the water.

When they finally took the beach Captain Miller, played by Tom Hanks, was given new orders from the top. He was to take seven of his best men and find a Private James Ryan, a paratrooper. Ryan's three brothers had been killed in other arenas on D-day and he was the only one left, so the war office felt that it was not right for a mother to lose all four of her sons in one war. The rest of the movie is a series of battles and heroic efforts to save the life of Private Ryan. Seven men die trying to bring Ryan home, and as the last man dies on a bridge he grabs Ryan's fatigues and says to him, "Earn this, seven men have died. Earn this."

Then Spielberg takes us to a graveyard where Ryan regularly visits those seven men who gave their lives for him and he says; "Every day I think about what you said during that day on the bridge. I've tried to live my life the best way I could. I hope it was enough. I hope at least in your eyes I've earned what all of you have done for me...tell me I have lived a good life...tell me I'm a good man."

Dan Koblosh saw this scene and in response wrote, "We Christians speak of 'owing' Christ for what He did for us, as we sing songs of unworthiness and feigned sorrow, yet we live lives of amazing selfishness and un-thankfulness."

I realize that this illustration has limits because nowhere in the Bible does Jesus say to 'earn this,' in fact you can't earn salvation; it's a free gift. But He does instruct us to be thankful and gracious. If a man can visit the graveyard of the men who died for him nearly every day surely we can visit the sanctuary of the God who has done so much more for us for more than one hour per week.

There is self-interest in this as well; best illustrated by Eric Liddell, the Scottish runner on whose life the movie *Chariots of Fire* is based.

After he had trained for four years for the Olympic one hundred meter race he discovered that the event was to be held on Sunday and Liddell decided he would not dishonor God by running on Sunday. Now you can argue about the ethics of running on Sunday but that's not the point. The point is that he felt that to run on Sunday would be to dishonor God and he wouldn't do that. He trained for four years, and he didn't run.

He went to the Scottish Olympic Committee and asked them to allow him to run the two hundred meters instead and they said yes. He was standing on the starting line on the day of the race, warming up, and Jackson Schultz, an American runner, came over and handed him a small piece of paper. Liddell opened it and read: 1 Samuel 2:30b "Those who honor me I will honor, but those who despise me will be disdained" (NIV). Liddell clutched that piece of paper, ran the two hundred meters of his life, and won the gold medal for his country.

I am not beyond needing the favor of God in my life, are you? God seems to say, "You honor me in worship and gratitude and be thankful for what you do have and stop looking at what you don't have. Honor me in gratitude and worship, get rid of this, 'God owes me a perfectly good life' attitude and I will honor you." At the moment you and I lose the sense of entitlement and begin thanking God for the things we have rather than complaining about the things we do not have, is the same moment we begin appreciating and recognizing God for who He truly is, the Giver of all good gifts. Then, maybe, just maybe, we will begin to pursue our relationship with God with the same passion that we pursued the things of this world prior to meeting Him. Thank God that He never gives us what we deserve. He has something so much better in mind.

CHAPTER 10

Where To From Here?

It's time to decide what you really believe. According to the Scriptures, very few people will actually choose to pursue God (see Matt. 7:14). They will be enticed by the lies of the world and eventually be caught up in the things of lesser value. Lesser loves will overcome them and one day they will find themselves not only living in a distant land far away from the Father but actually calling it home.

Remember, the author of over two-thirds of the New Testament categorically stated that everything he had seen or accomplished in this world was now rubbish, a dung heap, compared to knowing Christ Jesus. If you truly want to know God in the way He seeks to be known, if its Divine Romance you are looking for, then you must decide to allow God to pursue you through every event, tragic or non-tragic, in your life, and two, you must follow Paul's advice, religiously. His pursuit of God involved the following:

> "Not that I have already obtained all this, or have already arrived at my goal, but I press on to take hold of that for which Christ Jesus took hold of me. Brothers and sisters, I do not consider myself yet to have taken hold of it. But one thing I do: Forgetting what is behind and straining toward what is ahead, I press on toward the goal to win the prize for which God has called me heavenward in Christ Jesus" (Philippians 3:12-14).

Stay with me. I know you have probably heard this passage dissected many times but stay the course and you will be richly rewarded.

I love passionate people. I always have. When I played high school basketball there was this one kid, Keith Turner, who loved basketball like most of us love vacations. A gym rat, he could never get enough of the game or time in the gymnasium. A small, wiry kind of guy, not many believed Turner had any real future in the game but all were inspired by his tenacity. During his freshman year, Keith Turner began doing a most peculiar thing. He began placing a white strip of athletic tape on the side of the back board, leaping continuously into the air until he could reach the tape with his finger tips ten times in a row. Upon the completion of the goal, he would then grab a step ladder, advance the white strip one inch higher and then repeat the process. Keith Turner did not merely do this from time to time but every single night at the gym, as long as the custodian would allow before turning off the lights and locking the doors. At first, we all laughed at him, especially when he told us the reasoning for such madness. "One day, I am going to dunk a basketball in a real game and the fans are going to applaud and you all will too!" Man did we laugh our heads off! "Why you little peep squeak. You'll be lucky to make the team next year!" was the thought running through our heads.

Keith never gave up, and, a funny thing happened. He started to grow. Man did he grow! Next thing you know the white piece of athletic tape is getting closer and closer to the rim, and then closer and closer to the square over the rim! And then, my senior year, when I was captain of the varsity basketball team, we were playing Sullivan Central in the regional Big Ten tournament and something very special happened. Late in the third quarter, I pulled down a rebound, pivoted toward the outside just like Coach Carver taught me, and then, spotted Keith Turner at mid-court waiting for the outlet pass with nothing but hardwood between him and the goal. At that point time seemed to slow down. Everyone on the bench knew what was about to happen, or not. Receiving the outlet pass and turning swiftly toward our home goal, Turner took five of six power dribbles and launched himself in the air with one thing in mind—a rim bending, earth shattering, acrobatic dunk! Overwhelmed by the moment, I found myself frozen in time watching intently as Turner covered the distance between the floor and the rim with such ease that he had room to spare. With his tall lanky frame and his huge powerful hands he brought Mr. Spalding down so hard that the crowd erupted and the game had to be stopped in order to return the basketball hoop to its original place. While most people in the crowd, even those on the opposing team, were applauding, caught up in appreciation for such power and athleticism, we seniors who had been with Keith Turner from the time he was a freshmen, witnessing his passion for a goal and diligently taking the steps necessary to achieve it, began to weep. Holding back the tears was impossible. We knew what it meant to him but greatly underestimated what it would do to us.

Passion is a fantastic thing when accompanied with intentionality, strategy, and intestinal fortitude. I remember reading a story about a guy in Kentucky who was passionate about keeping his dog within the confines of the family farm. He purchased a dog collar that would fire electric shocks into the dog if he wandered too far from the property. Not wanting to take any chances, he decided to try the collar out for himself. In search of the right amount of voltage necessary to deter the dog from wandering too far, he tied the collar around his neck, gave his wife the controls and told her to increase the voltage every time she heard the sound of the car horn. So, he drove away from the home onto the main road and pressed down on the horn. The first level of charge was so violent that it caused him to swerve into oncoming traffic. At that point, everyone on the road began to engage their horns in disapproval. You can only imagine what was going on back at the farmhouse. Thinking that the husband is growing impatient with his wife's delinquency, she turns the device to full power. He suffered third degree burns and was rushed to the hospital. Unbridled passion usually results in disaster.

If your desire is to know God the way He seeks to be known and to experience all the byproducts that come with that, then here is where you begin. First, you must "strain toward what is ahead" (Phil 3:13). "It takes two to tango" is a popular phrase referring to the responsibility of both parties in any endeavor. God, through general revelation and specific occurrences in our lives has set about the process of courting us from the time we breathed our first breath. However, a relationship involves two people. Again, we are told that we will find God when we seek Him with all of our hearts. Discovering the God of the universe is not a once for all experience. It is something that you must be committed to. You must decide that you are going to raise the bar inch by inch until the good thing you are pursuing becomes reality. The apostle Paul said that what he wanted most in his life, beyond any other pursuit, was to "know Jesus" (Philippians 3:10). Then in Philippians 3:12-14 he describes the process by which this knowledge comes. "I press on to take hold. . ." (3:12).

People who accomplish great things have this one thing in common. They believe that direction, not intention, determines destination. Just because you want a successful marriage does not mean that you will have one. You must get on the road that leads to such a destination. Just because you want good kids who love God and serve Him with their whole heart does not mean that you will raise such kids. You gotta get on the road that leads to such a reality. Think of Mother Teresa for a moment. She was able to achieve great strides in mercy and compassion on the streets of Calcutta. Yet, an entry into her journal near the end of her life read, "May I truly obey you, starting today, to be a courier of your love and your grace to a hurting world. Because up to now, I have really done nothing." How can she possibly believe that? She had already done so much. This is what high achievers do. With each new day comes a fresh desire in their hearts to know God and to serve Him well. They possess a never-ending passion, an all-consuming objective to raise the level of excellence in their lives! They have a firm grasp on the reality that "little by little makes a bundle," as the African proverb communicates. So they pursue God every single day in hopes of one day arriving at an indescribable destination

After the Second World War Japan's economy was in disarray. Anything made in Japan was immediately discarded or at least seen as inferior. America sent in one of its best quality control experts in Dr. Edwards Deming. Seated before some of the best minds in Japan he stated the following, "If you will improve something about yourself and your product everyday, and make quality not something that like a threshold that you grab and hold onto but make improving or quality just part of your DNA, just part of your genetic make-up, and you just improve something everyday about yourself and your product, or what you produce or what you do, then here is my promise: within ten years you will turn the economy of Japan around and in thirty years you will be a world economic power." Simple advice yet profoundly effective. Japan bought Deming's words hook, line and sinker and in thirty years became a world power, economically speaking. Passionate people raise the bar, everyday, just a little. And then one day, the crowd stands in awe when they see the slam dunk you've always had inside.

What does that look like pragmatically in your life? What does a life that seeks to know God in the way He seeks to be known really look like? First, the manner in which a person responds to tragedy changes significantly. Rather than seeing such circumstances as God's abandonment they now see everything as God's divine courtship, revealing more of Himself through the tragedies of our lives while often stripping our lesser loves, those things that distract us from the pursuit of God. Second, and equally important, the life that pursues God goes hard after God with each new day believing that little by little God reveals more and more of Himself. So, each new day brings an opportunity to spend a bit more time in reading the Word, a little bit more time praying and seeking God, a little bit more time meeting with an accountability partner who speaks truth into your life. You know you are pursuing God when you don't just pray and read the Bible when you "feel" like it or are in trouble. The spiritual disciplines become a regular part of each new day because you understand the principle of "little by little makes a bundle" and you are committed to the long haul.

Not only do those who seek to truly know God raise the bar just a little bit every day, they also have an uncanny ability to forget the past. Past failures lose their ability to stifle future success. This is a learned art. Most of us suffer from the fear of failure, at least to some degree. As we get older we become less willing to take risks because every time we considered a new and exciting endeavor in the past, we came away frustrated and defeated. We remember the last diet or exercise program that we tried and the reality that we only lasted about six weeks before packing it all in. Part of the problem stems from the fact that we are not truly convinced that our efforts make any real or lasting difference. If we could go to the end and see what we will look like at the end of the journey, we would be more apt to endure. But this is the point. We have an absolute promise from God that when we seek Him with all of our hearts, we will find Him and begin to know Him as He seeks to be known. We all fail. We all make commitments that we fail to keep. But if you remember the covenant God made with Abraham in the very beginning of this book, you will also remember that God is absolutely committed to revealing Himself to us in the Divine Romance. If we will remain true to the course, getting back on the horse when we fail, trusting that although we often slide backwards, as long as we keep marching toward home, we will eventually arrive.

The alternative is disastrous and according to the Bible is the road more often traveled. A life that refuses to take risks for fear of failure is a mediocre, mundane life that looks nothing like the abundant life Jesus came to bring. Moreover, we miss out on a lifetime of fantastic, breath-taking adventures.

For instance, on our way to Thailand we decided to stop in Hong Kong for a few days. The first time I saw Hong Kong was in 1992 when Robin and I were on our way back to the United States for a respite from our work in Zimbabwe. Robin had always wanted to shop the late night markets downtown Hong Kong and I had always wanted to play the Royal Hong Kong Golf Club.

As soon as we landed we started searching for food. Robin wanted to walk through the streets and try the local quisine. I just wanted to find the golden arches! Robin asked, "Why on earth would you want to eat at a bad restaurant when you could enjoy foreign culinary delights?" I responded, "Because at least at McDonalds I know what I am getting: bad food! When I get the bad food I will not be disappointed. However, If I try some local food, expecting to enjoy the endeavor but instead finding that my taste buds have somehow been violated, I will suffer great disappointment. So, if its all the same to you, I'll just stick with what I know is bad rather than risk eating something bad that I had hoped would be good." She looked at me with a look I have seen many times since. It can be translated, "idiot." This most recent trip through Hong Kong was different. I am twice the age I was in 1992 and have learned to take great risks. As we began to try the local food, enjoying all the rich flavors, I just kept thinking of all that I had missed twenty-five years ago.

Eileen Gruder places this all in perspective when she writes:

> "You can live on bland food so as to avoid an ulcer, drink no tea, coffee or other stimulants in the name of health, go to bed early, stay away from night life, avoid all controversial subjects so as never to give offense, mind your own business, avoid involvement in other people's problems, spend money only on necessities and save all you can.
>
> You can still break your neck in the bath tub, and it will serve you right."

> (Eileen Gruder, quoted in *If You Want to Walk on Water,*
> *You've Got to Get Out of the Boat*, John Ortberg, p. 20)

True, isn't it? No matter how much you try to protect yourself at the plate, sooner or later you are going to get decked by an inside fastball. You might as well go down swinging!

The life that strives for greatness is the only life worth living, and, there is nothing greater than searching for and finding the God who longs to love you with an unconditional love that gives you every good and perfect gift.

For some of you, you have been traveling down the road of mediocrity for most of your life. You haven't changed anything about yourself for years! You need to comb your hair, buy some new clothes, maybe change your deodorant, anything new. Stop allowing your past to impact your future. So you tried life with God before and failed miserably. Okay, even that was part of your journey with God, so, embrace it, learn from it, and for heaven's sake, move on!

I don't know if you are familiar with Lee Kuan Yew, Singapore's Prime Minister. He singlehandedly restored Singapore to its former glory after the war. He took control of an international city on the verge of bankruptcy and poverty. In the midst of economic crises, he moved in with an unparalleled passion and vigor to get things moving forward again.

He established International Central Banking Systems with the vision that Singapore would become the tourist capitol of Asia. He made education available to the masses. He created low-income housing for the masses so that every man and woman willing to work could own their own home and have easy access to a quality education. Not all of his ventures succeeded and he received criticism for almost anything and everything he tried to accomplish. But, in the end, Lee Kuan Yew lived by one simple motto, "Get up! Get over it! Get going!"

Can I encourage you to do the same? When you fail, go home, repent, confess, but make sure you get up the next morning, lace up your basketball shoes, run down the court, and leap for the backboard—all over again!

This principle actually applies to every walk of life but especially to life with God. Your failures have been paid for. You stand in no condemnation concerning past sins and mistakes. You have absolute freedom to begin pursuing the God who has been pursuing you all of your life. Read His word, little by little every day. When the sin that so easily entangles you rears its ugly head, understand that you may never defeat it once and for all, you don't have to. Just try to be victorious over it in one twenty-four hour period at a time, and suddenly, one day, you will wake up to the realization that it no longer has power over you.

Forgiveness works the same way. Forgiving someone who has gravely offended you once and for all is a daunting challenge at best, but, if you can forgive that person one day at a time, next thing you know, the days have stacked together and its been months since you even thought about the violation committed against you. This is how victories come. One twenty-four hour period at a time. Indeed, "little by little does make a bundle."

So, reach forward toward the mark and forget past failures. This is the will of God. Take a closer look at your anatomy. God created you in a particular fashion to remind you to keep moving forward. Consider your eyeballs. They are in the front of your head, right? Now look at the way your ears lean forward and your feet point in a similar direction. Finally, notice how your arms move forward as your legs advance to take territory. There is only one part of your anatomy that is stuck on the other side and that just proves that God intended some things to be left behind! So get up, get over it and get going.

CHAPTER 11

One Final Note: "It Ain't Over Till It's Over!"

Well, wouldn't you know it? Before I could even finish writing this book, disaster strikes! Robin and I had just returned from our trip up the California coast when I decided to go for a bike ride along my favorite route adjacent to the 210 freeway here in San Bernandino County, CA. I was trekking along enjoying my ride when suddenly something told me to hit the brakes. Next thing I know I am in the back of an ambulance answering basic questions (What is your address? What year is this? What is your birth date?) from the paramedic. Fading in and out I finally come to full awareness in the San Bernandino Head Trauma Center. That's right! I am in the ER being told that I have broken both arms, suffered an eye socket fracture and need to be checked for internal cranial damage.

Finally, at 2 a.m. the doctors send me home insisting that I return in one week for further analysis. To make a long story short I ended up in two arm casts experiencing severe nausea from the concussion and the drugs needed to relive the pain. Amazing isn't it? I don't really know what caused the accident. Evidently, I blacked out before striking the pavement head-on. At any rate, I ended up incapacitated for the next eight weeks and restricted from any rigorous activity for the next three months. Ouch! During that time, I had plenty of time to think about what I wanted to write in this book. Better still, as I have believed for many years now, these are times when

God slows us down to reveal yet another part of Himself He needs and wants us to embrace in order that we may be effective servants of the kingdom of God.

What am I learning about God during this time? I am learning how fragile life really is. The doctors told me that accidents of this nature often result in paralysis of some kind. I am one of the lucky ones, or blessed one, depending on how you look at it. The reality is that there are no gurantees for any of us in this life. If we don't live our lives for a purpose outside and greater than ourselves, we will lose every time.

When I lived and worked in New Zealand I would often cross the pacific into Honolulu to visit one of the fastest growing churches in America at that time. Wayne Cordeiro pastored a rather large congregation that held its services at Farrington High School. During one of the meetings I witnessed Cordiero stand before his people holding a steel bar three feet long and three inches in diameter. With the level of his voice increasing with each phase of the illustration, he held the bar up high and proclaimed, "This bar of steel is worth about six dollars, however, if you convert it into cutlery, knives, forks, and spoons, the bar's worth increases to about sixty dollars." Cordeiro continued to elevate his voice as he fired off again, "But if you were to take this bar of steel and invest it into sewing needles, then guess what? This bar of steel is worth six hundred dollars." With people applauding Cordeiro interrupted, "But friends, if you take this same bar of steel and invest it into Swiss Watch springs, this lowly bar of steel will be worth six million dollars!" With a stunned crowd looking toward the stage their pastor asked, "What changed its worth? That in which it was invested!"

During this time away from my pulpit I have been spending time with God again and He has been revealing to me that perhaps it is time to give everything I have to His kingdom. Both my kids are out of the house and doing well. My wife and I are experiencing the empty nest syndrome, eating out more and going to sleep earlier. I've never had as much free time on my hands as I do now. I have been thinking of working on my golf swing and maybe playing in the club championship. Other things have been crossing my mind lately. These lesser loves, although not inherently evil or morally wrong, can often be distractions from the things that really matter. Through this season of my life I am gearing up for the final frontier of knowing God in the way He seeks to be known and am discovering that the method in which God is choosing to reveal Himself to me is in my service to others instead of serving myself in my later years. This morning, as I was reading my favorite devotional by Chris Tiegeen, I came across these words,

"A genuine appreciation of what Jesus did for us in His incarnation, death, and resurrection is just the beginning. His ministry is not just a beautiful event that we can admire for its wisdom and for the salvation it brings us. It also has practical implications for us. Looking back at that divine descent from glory to corruptible flesh, from self-existing life to a humiliating death, the disciples were to be struck with a personal realization: we are to do as He did. Jesus took off His respectable clothes and wrapped Himself in a servant's towel. He washed the dirtiest part of the human body in a semi-arid climate and a pedestrian culture. There is nothing glorious about cleaning feet. There is no recognition to be had there, no accolades for a great accomplishment. The disciples had surely had their feet washed before—by "real" servants—and had likely never even thanked them. Why should they? They were only doing what servants are obligated to do. Jesus spotted the dirtiest, most thankless area of physical need for the disciples and met it as an illustration of His mission. Then He got up and told the disciples that they should behave in exactly the same way. How often do we consciously do acts of service that others consider meaningless and unworthy of their talents? How often do we approach the needs of this world with a self-emptying attitude that will stoop as low as those needs demand? It goes against our human nature, doesn't it? We're always striving to work our way up, not work our way down. We think if we can attain to a higher status we can impact more people for the kingdom of God. Perhaps so, sometimes. But Jesus' example might lead us in another direction—farther down. Lower. Toward less glory. With less recognition. According to the Savior, that's the way to greatness in God's kingdom. As strange as this behavior seems, it's how He saved us. And it's how others will be saved. Jesus calls us to do as He has done for us. (July 25).

I am learning something very important where the pursuit of God is concerned. Here is how you know you are getting to know Him in the way He seeks to be known. You are becoming like Him. Just as Paul said, "I want to know Christ and the fellowship of sharing in His sufferings," so too you and I can know we are making progress toward God when we begin living less for ourselves and more for others.

GO HARD AFTER GOD

Can I ask you one final question? In what are you investing your life? Are you pursuing God or bigger and bigger barns? Are you living for others or are you living for yourself. I am trying to pass on to you what God has shown to me through twenty-seven years of ministry. You have a slam dunk in you! There is so much more to your life than all of these lesser loves for which you are living. Turn away from these idols and go hard after God. Little by little, day after day, reach out to Him. Give Him permission to do whatever it takes to make Himself known in your life. Ask the Master of the universe to touch you in such a way as to bring the real, authentic you to the surface, the one Christ has been occupying for some time now, the one who desires God more than anything else in this world. And while you give Him such permission, board the boat, hoist the sails, and get ready for the ride of your life!

A SPECIAL NOTE
TO PASTORS AND LEADERS

It has taken me thirty-two years of ministry to learn something I wish I had known far sooner in my preaching and teaching and leading career. You cannot manipulate and coerce people into living righteous lives of service and obedience to God. Yet, so much of our energy is spent trying to do just that. We spend hours trying to come up with clever homilies attempting to motivate our parishioners to tithe, serve, sign up for small groups, and a variety of other activities that are evidences of truly devoted followers of Jesus Christ. But here is an invaluable lesson to learn. The real issue is that many have not yet fallen in love with Jesus.

Interestingly enough, no one had to instruct me to talk about, serve, love, enjoy, give, sacrifice for or think about my wife Robin when I first fell in love. All of these things seemed to be the natural byproduct of falling in love with someone. I spent the majority of my resources on this new object of my affection. I gladly sacrificed my own wants and desires in order to be with her, talk to her, and learn everything I could about her. When you truly fall in love, the mind, emotions, and the will focus on the one thing you love most.

During the writing of this book, the light came on for me. I have truly changed the manner in which I approach the people whom God has entrusted to my care. My job is far more simple than I have made it. My responsibility is not to convict people of sin, righteousness, and judgement. Jesus said the Holy Spirit will do that and will do it much better than I ever could. My job is to simply keep giving the people of Christ's Church of the Valley the One thing they can't live without …

Jesus. The more I present the Jesus of the Scriptures, the more they will fall in love with Him. The more they fall in love with Him, the more these other issues will take care of themselves. The real issue in our churches is that our people are not yet in love with Jesus. They may respect Him, honor Him, even obey Him, but this is not the same thing as loving Him.

When you truly love Jesus, you do much more than appease Him, you actually desire to please Him. Appeasement results from reluctant, begrudging, temporary service. Ah! But true love stirs a dedication and commitment that is unparalleled in any of our other relationships. Help your people fall in love with Jesus and they will talk about Him, serve Him, obey Him, far more intensely and passionately than you could ever hope, dream, or imagine.

ABOUT THE AUTHOR

Pastor Jeff Vines spent twenty years on the mission field planting churches and training leaders (10 years in Zimbabwe and 10 years in New Zealand). From 1998-2005 he was the featured speaker on the weekly television broadcast, "Questions of Life," and frequently debated agnostic and atheist alike on national radio. For two years Jeff served as the Teaching Pastor at Savannah Christian Church in Savannah, GA. On January 1, 2008, Jeff became the Lead Pastor of Christ's Church of the Valley in San Dimas, CA. Jeff is the author of *Dinner with SKEPTICS: Defending God in a World That Makes No Sense* (2008, 2011) and *Unbroken: 8 Enduring Promises God Will Keep* (2012). Jeff and his wife, Robin, celebrated their 30th anniversary in July of 2016 and have two children, Delaney and Sian.